The Book of Life

THE NEW TESTAMENT RETOLD

The Book
of Life

BY
HENRI DANIEL-ROPS

TRANSLATED BY DONAL O'KELLY
ILLUSTRATED BY FRITZ KREDEL

An
ARKIVE
EDITION
FROM ⚜ SOPHIA INSTITUTE PRESS

Sophia Institute Press®
Box 5284, Manchester, NH 03108
1-800-888-9344
www.SophiaInstitute.com

The Book of Life is a translation of *L'Evangile de mes Filleuls*
by Henri Daniel-Rops (Paris, La Colombe, 1955) originally published
in English in 1956 by P. J. Kenedy & Sons, New York.

Nihil Obstat: Joannes J. O'Rourke, S.T.L., L.S.S.,
Censor Deputatus Philadelphia, Pa., June 23, 1956

Imprimatur: ✠ J. F. O'Hara, C.S.C.,
Archbishop of Philadelphia, July 16, 1956

Library of Congress Cataloging-in-Publication Data

Daniel-Rops, Henri, 1901-1965.
  [Evangile de mes filleuls. English]
  The Book of Life : the New Testament Retold / by Henri Daniel-Rops ;
translated by Donal O'Kelly ; illustrated by Fritz Kredel. — Arkive ed.
      p. cm.
  ISBN 978-1-933184-49-4 (ppbk : alk. paper) 1. Bible. N.T.—History of
Biblical events. I. O'Kelly, Donal. II. Title.

BS2407.D3613 2009
225.9'5—dc22
                              2009009133

      09 10 11 12 13 14 10 9 8 7 6 5 4 3 2 1

Contents

Contents

Map Endpapers

The Book of Life

How the Good News Was Made Known to the World

NIGHT WAS FALLING on Rome and already, in the warm clear twilight, the evening star shone over the not far distant sea. Hand-in-hand two children, a boy of thirteen and a girl of twelve, made their way toward one of the city gates. At first glance, one would have taken them for two children trying to escape from the heat of the city for a walk in the surrounding countryside. But, if this were so, why did they seem so much on their guard and why did they glance quickly and with distrust at those who passed them by, as though they were afraid of being pursued?

After the pair had followed the great main road, paved with large stone blocks, for well over a mile, they turned off and ran quickly toward a cypress grove. There, screened from the road, was the opening to a narrow sloping corridor that led underground. They went down the steps without any fear, for they knew it would lead them into the company of friends. Soon they saw the glimmer of an oil lamp at the end of the gallery, where it opened out into a vaulted chamber. Coming toward them was an old man who recognized them at once, and raised his hands in a gesture of great concern. "May the Lord protect you, my little ones," he said, to which they replied, "May our Divine Master be with you."

"The meeting is about to begin and Mark himself is with us tonight, so come quickly," the old man said. The children made haste toward the chamber where many voices were raised in a song that they knew well.

What was this secret meeting all about and who were these people who came together in an underground chamber to sing strange songs? Why had the two children taken such care to see that no one was following them?

All this took place about nineteen centuries ago, at the beginning of our Christian era. In those days, as you know from your history books, the Western world, consisting of the countries bordering on the Mediterranean Sea, was under the rule of the Roman emperors. They knew how to rule, those emperors, and their territory was well organized and governed, with fine roads everywhere. There was law, order, peace and prosperity throughout the vast empire. But the Romans were still pagans, that is, they adored all sorts of strange gods: the forces of nature, the sky, the sea, the wind and the lightning, to all of which they gave names and in whose honor they erected statues before which they performed ceremonies and offered sacrifices—as though this could be of any avail!

However, even among the Romans themselves there were many wise and thoughtful people who could find no comfort in their religion, for they could not bring themselves to believe that idols of stone and gilded wood, made by the hands of men, could really be divine. They also were of the opinion that the stories told by the Greeks of their gods in books called "mythologies," while often amusing, were not very edifying. Such people were, therefore, uneasy in their minds. And now for some time past men had been appearing here and there throughout the empire who declared that the Roman religion was false. "Your idols," they said, "are nothing but the wood, plaster and stone of which you made them. These innumerable forces of nature which you hail as gods are but expressions of the power of the One True God, the God who made the universe, the earth and the human beings who dwell on it. We have come to bring you tidings that the True God Himself has come down to earth, to teach truth and peace to men." More and more the pagans were listening to this message and in increasing numbers were becoming converted to the new religion.

Now we can easily understand that the Roman emperors did

not like this state of affairs at all. What would happen, they asked, if all their subjects abandoned the official religion and refused any longer to believe in the gods of Rome? So they began to persecute the believers in the new religion. These were tracked down by the imperial guard, and when any were captured it meant imprisonment, hard labor and sometimes even death by horrible tortures. This persecution forced the believers in the new religion to practice their faith in secret and to hold their meetings in underground chambers called the Catacombs. It was just such a meeting to which our young boy and girl were hastening, for their parents, alas, had been arrested by the imperial guards, and their fellow believers were very troubled about their fate. The children, however, with the bravery of youth, continued to attend the secret meetings: it never crossed their minds that they should be unfaithful to the teachings of their father and mother. And if anyone had asked them why they were there and why they risked arrest and imprisonment, we can be quite sure that they would have proudly answered what their parents had taught them from birth, "Because we, too, are Christians."

Let us now join the meeting to which we have been led by our two little friends, our brother and sister of so long ago. Huddled close together, for there was not much room in this cavern, the congregation was praying and singing aloud. The words that sprang to their lips are very well known to us all: "I believe in God, the Father Almighty, Creator of heaven and earth," or perhaps: "Our Father who art in heaven, hallowed be Thy name." One of their number, a venerable old man, took bread, blessed it, and raised it aloft, at the same time pronouncing slowly certain words. He then distributed a piece of the bread to each member of the assembly. After this a man stood up before them, and a profound silence reigned as he spoke.

"My dear brethren," he cried, "of whom shall I speak to you but of Him, and Him only? I who stand before you am called Mark, an unworthy witness of our Divine Master. I was but a youth while He lived on earth and afterward I labored at the side of Peter, the leader of His disciples. It is from Peter and His other companions that I have learned what I know and what I am now about to tell you.

"And who is this whose miracles and example I am going to recount and whose words I am about to repeat to you? You all know: He was a man like you and me, known to other men, who died as we all must die. But this man was God, the True God, the Son of God. Here is a mystery beyond our understanding! The Almighty God on whom depends everything in this world, not merely on this earth but beyond the farthest star that you can see in the sky, willed it that His Son, that is to say Himself, should take a human form like ours and come to dwell among us. But why? So that men might hear from a human voice the words that would enlighten them for all time. So that they might learn how they should live and, above all, so that they should learn to love one another. . . . And you know the name of this God-Man, this bearer of good tidings. . . ."

With one voice the congregation cried aloud, "Jesus."

So the meeting continued, and we can imagine how earnestly the two children listened to what was being said. Jesus, yes, it was He of whom their mother had spoken ever since they were able to understand her. Jesus, also called Christ from the Greek word *Christos,* meaning "consecrated by God." (It is from this name that the followers of Jesus were called Christians.) They knew that Jesus was the sole model for them to follow: Jesus, whose life was full of marvels and whose lips spoke only words of holiness and consolation. So they listened with all their ears as Mark told them about Him:

"At that time, Jesus was with His disciples on a ship on the lake in His country. And there arose a great storm of wind, and the waves beat into the ship, so that the ship was filled. And He was in the back part of the ship, sleeping upon a pillow. His disciples awakened Him, saying, 'Lord, save us, we perish.' And rising up, He rebuked the wind and said to the sea, 'Peace, be still.' And the wind ceased and there was made a great calm, so that the disciples said, one to another, 'Who is this, that both wind and sea obey Him?' "

People never tired of hearing stories like this and hundreds of others like it. The most wonderful and beautiful thing about them was that they not only told of events in the life of Jesus but they used His very own words: "Love one another. . . . Forgive, and you will be forgiven. . . . Do good to them that hate you. . . ." These teachings and many others had been expressed by Jesus in phrases that were short and simple but unforgettable. Each one who heard these stories about Him felt a strange change: he became purer, better, and more warm of heart. It was as though a ray of light had struck to the depths of his soul, bringing such a sense of peace and consolation that he longed to be able to preserve it forever.

So deep was the impression made on the two children on this

night that as they made their way back from the secret meeting in the Catacombs to the house where they hoped to find their parents again, they said to one another, "Surely, we will soon have a book in which all these wonders will be written down, perhaps a copy of our very own, that we will be able to read and reread whenever we want to. Such a book will tell of all the wonderful happenings in Jesus' life and all the things He said. The people who had the happiness of knowing Him during His life on earth must write down for us everything they know. What a beautiful book it will be!"

The book for which those Christian children longed so many years ago *was* written, and today we know it well. In our country no courage is needed in order to declare our faith in Jesus Christ, and if we want to know more about Him, we do not have to hide, to go secretly to underground meeting places. But all the same, the stories of His life are no less wonderful now than they were in the early days, and His words have the same appeal as they had then. Nineteen centuries have passed since, but when we read of the acts of our Divine Lord we still feel in our hearts the same warmth as did the early Christians. This book, which tells of the actions and repeats the words of Jesus, is the most precious possession of the human race.

It is called the Gospel, a word which means "Good News." Good news indeed! It is the message which Jesus brought to mankind and the example which He set for all of us to follow. It contains the gladdest tidings that ever reached this earth. If only men had listened to the message, how much better the world would be and how much less would it be filled with suffering, cruelty and violence!

This book came to be written exactly as our two young early Christian friends hoped it would be. Each time the first Christian communities were visited by someone who had known Jesus or had been in close touch with one of His disciples, they begged him to tell them of the Master, just as we have seen Mark do. The people listened with rapt attention, treasuring every word and repeating what they had heard to others.

In the beginning, therefore, the Good News was passed along by word of mouth. These first Christian missionaries sometimes had written notes, but it soon became clear that these were not sufficient and could not contain everything. There was also the danger that the evidence of those who had actually known Christ might be forgotten or altered as it was handed on. Because of this, people in every Christian community asked, as we heard our young friends ask, for a book in which everything known about Christ would be written down.

Then God, the Almighty God who watches over and guides the works of man, decided that the time had come when the Good News should be set down in writing. He inspired the four men whom we now call the "Four Evangelists" to undertake the task.

The first to start was Matthew, an actual disciple of Jesus; he had known Him intimately and had lived by His side during the wonderful adventure of His life and death on earth. It was not difficult for Matthew to write down what he knew so well, and he completed his task sometime between the years A.D. 50 and 55. In his Gospel he devoted himself particularly to recording the words of the Master as accurately as he could.

When Matthew had finished his task, another man read what he had written and found that he could add much to it. This was Mark, whom we have already met preaching in the Catacombs. The disciple and friend of St. Peter, the chief of the Apostles, Mark was also well informed. Peter had told him all he knew about the Master, particularly of His actions and the most important events of His life. Between the years 55 and 62, Mark set down in writing this further testimony to be added to what Matthew had already written.

A little later a highly-cultured Greek, a physician called Luke, seeing how the Christian faith was spreading more and more in Greek and Roman circles, thought it would be a good thing to prepare a version of the Gospel especially for these people. So in the year A.D. 63, Luke produced his version, beautifully written in terms that would appeal to educated people. Besides, Luke had known Our Lady, the mother of Jesus, very well, and so he was able to give us original and delightful glimpses of the Master's childhood.

Finally, and very much later, a fourth part was added to the existing three parts. It was the work of John, the youngest and most beloved of the disciples of Jesus. He had been very young when Christ lived on earth, and now, in extreme old age, about the year A.D. 100, the thought came to him, "I must not let death take me before I have written down what I have heard with my own ears, before I leave to men the words the Master spoke to me when I rested my head on His shoulder." And so, although he was then nearly a hundred years old, God gave John the strength to write a fourth text which beautifully completed the work of the other three Evangelists.

And that was how there came into being what we call the Gospel, that is, all of the texts written by the four Evangelists, St. Matthew, St. Mark, St. Luke and St. John. These four texts make a complete whole, sometimes repeating each other, but on certain points each adding details not included in the other three. They are all parts of the same book and form one body of teaching: the Good News brought to the world by Jesus Christ.

You see now how fortunate we are to possess this wonderful little book which brings to us so much light and truth. Every time you go to church on Sunday you hear an extract from the Gospel, but we should also follow it from beginning to end, for it is all beautiful and there is not a word in it that is not of value to us. It is of the whole Gospel that I am going to tell you in this book, and I am quite sure that as you read it chapter by chapter you will listen to its message with the same zeal and interest as if you had been listening to it in the secret depths of the Catacombs almost nineteen hundred years ago.

II

The Child Jesus Is Born

"Mary, Mary!" The young girl, quietly working in her room, started with surprise and turned around quickly. She did not recognize the wonderfully gentle and musical voice that called her by name. As her eyes turned toward the open door, she was still more startled. There, framed in the door and right beside her, was a huge, shining figure, so dazzling that it seemed to be now a wonderfully graceful young man, now a great swan with down-swept wings, and now just a dancing ray of sunlight. As she stood rooted to the ground, but filled with a happiness she could not understand, the full, gentle voice spoke again, "Hail, full of grace, the Lord is with thee."

This happened at Nazareth, in Galilee—a strange place for such an event to take place. At this time Augustus, the first and greatest of its emperors, ruled Rome, and the entire Western world looked only to him. Most certainly no one had a glance to spare for Nazareth in Galilee, a tiny province of Palestine, itself the smallest of the emperor's dominions (see map at front of book). Even in Galilee, Nazareth did not count for much, for it had been for centuries only a mountain hamlet of workers and peasants. No one would ever have guessed that here, in a lost corner of a forgotten country, an event was to take place far more important than any decision made by Augustus in his marble palace. The human mind cannot understand the working of God's will.

To the eyes of men, there was nothing very exceptional about the young girl who had been singled out for this strange visit. She was about fifteen years old, and her parents, Joachim and Anne, were simple, honest working people. The name she bore was in common use in Palestine. In making her His choice, God had another surprise for the world, for who ever dreamed that this little Nazarene girl would become the greatest woman of all time, whose name, two thousand years later, would be daily on the lips of millions of human beings? Only God Himself, who reads the innermost hearts of men, saw the infinite purity, goodness, faith and piety in the soul of Mary of Nazareth. In her whole life, she had never committed sin, and her soul had always been completely spotless. It was because of this that God had sent her this mysterious winged messenger, who was in fact an angel, one of those invisible beings who surround the throne of God for all eternity.

He was Gabriel, one of the foremost angels in the court of heaven, whose name means "Power of God." And now his voice continued, "Fear not, Mary. You are blessed among women, and I bring you great tidings. Soon you will have a son and you shall call His name Jesus. He shall be great, for He shall be the Son of the Most High. All power will be given to Him by God, and of His reign there shall be no end."

As she listened to these words, Mary was more than astonished. Who had ever heard that God Himself would have a Son or that a child could be called "Son of the Most High?" Mary did not know in advance that the Almighty God had resolved to come to earth, that He wished to live as a man and to be born of a mother as all men are. None of this was known to Mary, but now Gabriel explained it to her. For a moment she remained silent, a young girl overwhelmed by the honor done to her and, in her humility, unable to understand very well why she had been chosen. But, all her life, she had known that there is but one rule, that is to obey the commands of God.

And so, lifting her eyes to the dazzling figure of the angel, she replied, "Behold the handmaid of the Lord, be it done to me according to Thy word. . . ."

The days passed by and all the while Mary pondered in her

heart on the angel's message. As she mused upon what he had said, she remembered that when Gabriel had announced to her the will of God, he had added, "If you wish proof that to God nothing is impossible, go and visit your cousin Elizabeth. As you know, she is very old, long past the age when people have children, but all the same, you will find that she is going to have a son."

After a while Mary decided that she would go to see Elizabeth. So she set off on the long road from Nazareth to the little Judean village of Ain Karim in Southern Palestine, where Elizabeth lived. After a journey of at least four days she arrived at her cousin's house, knocked at the door, and was warmly greeted. All that the angel had said was true. The aged Elizabeth, who all her life had longed for a child, was now, by the special grace of God, about to have a son. Gabriel was right: nothing is impossible to God.

At the very moment when Mary and her cousin met face to face, the power of God was once more made clear. Before a word of explanation could be spoken, Elizabeth knew why Mary had come to see her and knew the message that she brought. She was overwhelmed with joy at the thought of God becoming Man, and that Mary was to be His Mother. In her delight she added to Gabriel's salutation the words, "Blessed art thou among women, and blessed is the fruit of thy womb. . . ."

A flood of heavenly light flowed into Mary's soul. It was all true then; everything that the angel had promised her was about to happen. Not merely was Elizabeth going to have a child as he had foretold but her cousin was now repeating the same things Gabriel had said to her. Mary could no longer restrain the emotion which filled her whole soul, and she burst into a song that was also a wonderful prayer:

"My soul doth magnify the Lord. And my spirit has rejoiced in God my Saviour. Because He has regarded the humility of His handmaid; for behold from henceforth all generations shall call me blessed. Because He that is mighty, has done great things to me. . . ."

On her return to Nazareth, Mary decided to tell her betrothed husband of the wonderful thing that had happened to her. She was already promised in marriage; in the East it is the custom for girls to marry at the age of fourteen or fifteen. Her husband-to-be was called Joseph, after the great Israelite hero of whose life and adventures in Egypt you have already read in the Old Testament. Mary's Joseph was a just and good man, very faithful to the law of God.

But he was very troubled by what Mary had to tell him. He could not understand it. What did it mean that Mary's son would be the Son of God? Surely, after they were married, her sons would be his. The whole thing seemed so strange that Joseph thought of breaking his betrothal.

But now it was Joseph's turn to be visited by an angel. "Fear not, Joseph, or try to question Mary any further, for it is God Himself who is the Father of her Son. Remember the words of the prophet, Isaias, that the Saviour will be 'born of a virgin.' That prophecy is now about to be fulfilled. Mary is the young girl, the holy virgin, who has been chosen by God to be His mother. And when the child is born, you shall call His name Jesus."

After the vision in which the angel spoke to him, Joseph knew what God wished of him. The tender Mary and her Divine Child would need the protection of a wise and good man who would be able to provide for them. God had called on him to play the humble but very necessary part of foster father and protector, and Joseph understood and accepted his duty. No doubt, in his secret heart, he echoed Mary's own reply to Gabriel, "Be it done to me according to thy word. . . ."

The time finally arrived which God had chosen for the birth of Jesus. And just at that time orders went out from the government for the taking of a census. You know what a census is: a list of all the inhabitants of a country—men, women and children. Such a list is very useful to the government when it comes to collecting taxes and calling men up for military service. The custom of taking a census prevails in all civilized countries, including our own.

But in Palestine in those far-off days, the method of taking the census was quite different from what it is today, when people do not have to leave their homes to answer the questions. Then, everyone had to return to their original family home and, even if this was far away, the journey had to be made.

Now, both Mary and Joseph belonged to the royal family of David, which came originally from Bethlehem, not far from Jerusalem. It may seem strange to you that this humble pair should be descendants of King David, the great hero and poet of Israel. But it is easy to understand how this came to be. David had many children, and in the thousand years that had gone by since his death not all his descendants had remained rich and prosperous. Many were simple, humble folk, and so it was with Mary and Joseph. They were truly of David's royal line but this did not prevent them from being poor.

It did mean, however, that on the day of the census they had to appear in Bethlehem to be enrolled, and this meant a very long journey (see map). Nevertheless, it was all part of God's plan. The Prophets, as you will remember, had long ago foretold that the Saviour to come would be a descendant of King David and would be born in Bethlehem. If the child was to see the light in Bethlehem because the census order had brought His parents there, here is still further proof that God's plan was unfolding and that this Child would be truly His Son.

All the same, it was a long and weary road Mary and Joseph were to follow, along the whole length of the Jordan valley, a matter of some seventy-five miles. After this the road climbed to Jerusalem and then continued south to Bethlehem. There was another possible road by Engannim and Sichem, but it was mountainous and meant climbs up and down the whole way. It would have taken five days on donkey-back, and would have been far too tiring for Mary.

When they finally arrived in Bethlehem, Mary was badly in

need of a rest. But the town was swarming with country people, all come to register at the census. She and Joseph tried to get into an inn on the outskirts of the town, the sort of noisy and uncomfortable place one still finds in the East, but it was packed to the doors with men, women, children and animals. They were not allowed to enter, and they turned away, very tired and perhaps a bit discouraged.

Fortunately, the limestone hills throughout Judea are pitted with caves of all sizes, many of which have been hollowed out by men and used by them to shelter their beasts. We see such stables to this day in Palestine, poor stables with straw scattered about and perhaps some straw in a manger cut out of the earthen walls. It was in one of these caves that Joseph, unable to find any better place, took Mary for shelter. It is likely he stabled their little donkey, their faithful traveling companion, in a corner of the cave, which may already have been sheltering cattle and sheep. For the descendants of King David this was not a very suitable dwelling. . . . But it was chosen by God as a great lesson to men: that He is to be found in poverty and humility, and that a pure and simple soul is more pleasing to Him than all the splendors of the earth.

On the hills near the cave where Joseph and Mary had taken shelter, shepherds were watching their flocks. It is the custom in the East, when the weather is not too cold, to leave the sheep in their pastures but, at the time of which we speak, wild animals were plentiful in Judea and the shepherds had to guard their flocks against wolves, jackals, and even lions. It was for this reason that they were on the hillside that night, calling out to each other from time to time to make sure that no one slept at his post, and now and then playing a tune on their pipes.

Suddenly these men found themselves bathed in light and from the skies a heavenly voice called to them, "Behold I bring you good tidings of great joy. Rejoice, for the Divine Child is born. Make haste to the stable in Bethlehem where a newborn babe lies asleep in a manger. It is He, the Saviour, the Son of God."

And while the shepherds made haste to the stable where Mary and Joseph bowed in adoration before the infant Son of God, the heavens were filled with angels' voices singing, "Glory to God in the highest; and on earth peace to men of good will."

III

Jesus Grows in Wisdom and Age

IN THESE DAYS, as you know, when a child is born its parents' first care is to have it baptized, that is, to dedicate it to God and to make it a Christian. In Israel at the time when Jesus came on earth, the birth of a child was also marked by important religious ceremonies. First of all, the child had to be given a name within a week of birth, and this name was chosen with due regard to family traditions and the child's future position in life. Then, forty days after birth, the parents had to bring the Babe to the Temple in Jerusalem to have him blessed by the priests.

There was no difficulty in choosing a name for Jesus, since Gabriel had told it in advance, and both Joseph and Mary were obedient to the command. The name of Jesus that is now to us such a wonderful one was in those days quite usual in Palestine. In choosing this almost commonplace name, God showed that He wished to appear on earth as an ordinary man, no different from the rest. The name, however, had also a very beautiful meaning which was "God saves."

On the appointed day, Joseph and Mary, carrying their little Son, climbed the steep way that led from the city to the Temple. They entered the huge courtyard that was always crammed with people who came to pray, to meditate or just to chat, and went in search of the priest who was to bless the Babe. But no sooner had they entered the Temple than God's Hand was again shown in a sudden and surprising way.

Among the crowd in the Temple, there was a very holy old man called Simeon. All his long life he had served God faithfully. Many times, in his prayers, he had asked God, "O Lord, must I die without seeing the Saviour foretold by the Prophets, the One sent by Thee to bring salvation to men?" Now, a secret voice spoke to him and directed his steps toward the humble couple who, with their Child, were making their way as best they could through the crowd. It said to him, "This is He, this is the Saviour." Not for an instant did Simeon doubt the truth of what he heard. Taking the infant Jesus in his arms he raised Him toward heaven while a prayer came from his heart: "Now, O Lord, let thy servant depart in peace; because my eyes have seen my Saviour, the Light which will shine upon all nations."

We now see the plan of the Almighty for the coming on earth of Jesus. It was His will that Jesus be born in humble modesty, not at all like a prince or king. But at the same time He permitted a few devout souls to guess the wonderful secret contained in the frail body of the newborn Babe. The holy Simeon, because he had prayed and hoped so much, was one of those to whom the mystery was revealed, so that before his death the future was known to him. Not all he foresaw was joyous. The old man knew the tragic fate in store for the Babe that now lay smiling in His mother's arms, and for a moment he trembled. Turning to Mary, he murmured gently, "And thine own soul a sword shall pierce. . . ." Mary, we can be sure, did not reply, but closed her eyes in prayer: had she not accepted utterly God's will toward her?

Another no less surprising event took place shortly afterward. Far away from Palestine, in countries where there were no Israelites, there were some very wise and scholarly men called "Magi" by the Persians. They were highly versed in the study of the stars. Three of these men, as they studied the movement of the stars in the clear skies of Asia, came to the conclusion that far away to the West an extraordinary event had taken place: the birth of a Child with a great destiny.

Following the guidance they had received, they started out toward the setting sun. We can picture for ourselves their great caravan of haughty camels, bedecked with costly trappings as was customary for the kings of the East. Day after day they traveled toward the West to the steady pace of their majestic beasts, and always before them shone the star that guided them on their way.

At last they reached Palestine and made inquiries as to where they could find the newborn Babe whose coming had been announced in the heavens. Their guiding star remained their faithful guide to the end, and it led them to the dwelling of Joseph, Mary and the Babe. As these men were deeply believing and knew the world to be ordered by the divine Will, it did not surprise them that the Almighty should have chosen such humble people to carry out His plan. They threw themselves at the feet of the Child Jesus and ordered their servants to unload from the camels the costly presents they had brought: gold, frankincense and myrrh. These they offered to Him.

Then they departed, pondering on the mystery of the power of God which had revealed to them the birth of God made Man.

Unfortunately, this visit of the Magi had an immediate and tragic result. As you know,[1] Palestine was at this time governed by a cruel tyrant placed on the throne by the Romans because they knew he would be obedient to them. This was a half-Arab called Herod, a strange and very wicked man. He had rebuilt the Temple of Jerusalem in magnificent style but at the same time he broke every law of God and committed all kinds of horrible sins. He had put to death his favorite wife, two of his sons, and several of his nephews, for he dreaded above all the thought that one day someone might deprive him of his power and his throne.

When the Magi arrived in Palestine they called on Herod out of politeness. Although they had no way of knowing precisely who the newborn child would be, they asked Herod, "Where is He that is born king of the Jews?" We can well imagine how this inquiry upset Herod. A king of the Jews! Another king but himself! At once he summoned his counselors and told them to find out just where in

[1] See *The Book of Books*, chapter xix.

Palestine the Prophets had foretold that the Messias would be born. Although Herod knew little of the Scriptures, he was crafty enough to guess that the Babe of whom the Magi spoke was the same whose birth had been foretold by Isaias, Daniel and the other great Hebrew Prophets of former days. "In Bethlehem," Herod's counselors told him. "It is foretold that the Messias will be born in Bethlehem."

When he heard this, Herod did not hesitate for a moment but issued a savage order: "Kill all the boys born in Bethlehem during the last two years." This was done, and so occurred the horrible slaughter of the innocents. At that time Bethlehem was a town of about two thousand inhabitants, so the victims must have numbered at least thirty; thirty little babies killed and thirty heartbroken mothers weeping over them.

But Jesus did not fall a victim to the tyrant, for an angel appeared and warned Joseph of what was about to happen. "Arise," he said, "and take the Child and His mother, and fly into Egypt. Stay there until I tell you. For it will come to pass that Herod will seek the Child in order to destroy Him." Joseph obeyed instantly, and traveling by day and by night, the Holy Family set out along the difficult and monotonous track across the desert of southern Palestine. Mary carried the Babe on a donkey, the good foster father tramping beside them. Several times they almost died of thirst, but finally they reached Egypt and settled down there until the danger that threatened them was past. As, in fact, Herod was called to account for his misdeeds before God a few months after his latest crime, Joseph soon heard from the angel that the death of the tyrant had removed all risk. He then took the road back to Palestine with Mary and the infant Jesus.

Our story must now bridge a gap of several years. Now we find the Holy Family once more at home, that is, in Nazareth. If ever you are fortunate enough to journey to the Holy Land, be sure to pay a visit there. Today, Nazareth is a good-sized village of white houses, lying in a circle of hills, built on terraces where the cypress trees stand tall and dark. All around are fields of wheat, vineyards and olive groves, and the air is heavy with the scent of flax and verbena. The walls of many of the houses are covered with the purple flowered creeper which is called bougainvillea.

It is against this setting that we must try to picture the Child for ourselves. Jesus "grew and waxed strong, full of wisdom; and the grace of God was in Him," as St. Luke puts it. In appearance, He was probably not very different from the little Jewish boys we still see in Palestine—lively, intelligent and clear-eyed.

We have practically no details of His daily life during the years of His childhood. But we can get a fair idea of the house in which He lived from the modest dwellings that we find there today, unchanged in design for the last two thousand years. This house must have consisted of only one or two rooms with white-washed walls, sparsely furnished, and poorly lit with earthenware oil lamps. Quite likely, His parents' house, as is still the custom of the country, was partly cut into the hillside and partly built up from without. A room somewhat larger than the others served as a workshop, for Joseph earned his living as an artisan.

As for Jesus, He spent His childhood days much as any other little Jewish boy of His time. He attended the synagogue, the place of assembly and prayer that existed in every Jewish village, and here He received a very thorough education. Seated on the ground in groups about their master, the pupils read from rolls of parchment or papyrus selected texts from the Bible. These taught them all that men of their period needed to know: their traditional tongue, Hebrew; God's commandments to Moses; the history of their race and its supernatural mission. After school hours Jesus played with His numerous cousins in the adjoining countryside, climbing to the summits of the nearby hills in the hope of catching a glimpse of the distant sea. In outward appearance Jesus was a boy just like all other boys, and yet there was in His heart a quality that made Him quite different from them.

How different He was is illustrated by a story told in St. Luke's

Gospel. Jesus was about twelve years old when His parents took Him with them to celebrate the feast of the Passover at Jerusalem, as was the custom of most pious Jews. Together they prayed in the Temple and they ate the roast lamb that was a traditional part of the celebration of the feast. Then they started for home in the company of many others, singing psalms on the way.

When they halted after their first day's journey, Jesus was missing, nor could He be found among their relatives and friends. None of them had seen Him. Joseph and Mary were naturally very anxious and hastened back to Jerusalem. For three days they searched for Him in vain. At last they found Him in the Temple, the center of a group of learned men called Scribes or Doctors of the Law, and He was discussing difficult points of religious doctrine with them. These wise men were amazed at the wisdom and knowledge displayed by the youth. In this happening we see proof that God's plans for this little boy were very different from those He had for all others.

Mary well knew the destiny of her Son, but what must she have thought when Jesus answered her reproaches for the anxiety He had caused her and Joseph? He said, "How is it that you sought Me? Did you not know that I must be about My Father's business?" She knew that the Father of whom He spoke was none other than the Almighty God.

And now we must leave Jesus in Nazareth to grow up from childhood, through His youth, until He became a mature man. The Gospel tells us nothing of these years, as if to point out the lesson that, in order to carry out the will of God, man must prepare for the task in humility and silence. This humble private life of Jesus throws into greater relief the period of His public life when He was to reveal Himself as the Messias.

When He was about fifteen, no doubt His foster father taught Him his own trade of carpentry, that noble craft that calls for so much skill and intelligence and without which we would have no

roofs over our heads. He was to be met in the streets, wearing behind his ear the wood shaving that was the badge of His trade. Or
He was to be found in His workshop, trimming wood with His adz
or hammering His timbers together. Joseph must have died some
time before Jesus grew to manhood, for the Gospel speaks no more
of him. Joseph's appointed task was finished; his foster son had
grown up and no longer needed a protector.

Jesus was about thirty years of age when His humble and hidden life came to an end and God called Him to begin His mission to
men.

IV

At the Ford of Bethany

OUR STORY MOVES from the smiling hillsides of Nazareth to the deep Jordan valley in southern Palestine. We are now in the most low-lying part of the country, for what is most unusual, the land lies as much as 1,300 feet below sea level. Here, in a long canyon surrounded by rocky cliffs, lie the sluggish waters of the Dead Sea, so salty and full of bitumen that no fish can live in them and a man can float on them without swimming. It is a desolate countryside of sun-scorched and arid land, a reminder of the evil cities of Sodom and Gomorrah which once stood on this spot and which God destroyed by fire from heaven.[1]

A short distance north of the Dead Sea, not far from where the River Jordan flows into it, there is a ford, that is, a place where the river is shallow and where it can be easily crossed. It is a pleasant spot, where the waters chatter gaily between banks lined with willows, oaks and mimosa shrubs. Although very hot in summer, the winter climate is delightful, particularly when a fresh breeze from the north stirs the evening air.

There is always a good deal of traffic at a ford, and this ford of Bethany was busier than most. All merchants and caravans traveling eastward from Jerusalem toward the desert routes leading to Mesopotamia or to Moab and Arabia had to cross the Jordan there. At the ford one met Jews, Bedouins, Arabs, Babylonians, Assyrians, Egyptians and African Negroes; men of all races and colors, so that it was a busy place at all times.

Toward the end of the year A.D. 27, the ford was even more frequented and bustling than usual. Many travelers whose business

[1] See *The Book of Books,* chapter II.

brought them that way remained instead of continuing their journey, while from all parts of Palestine men and women rushed to the ford and stayed about for days and days. Finally a great crowd had gathered as though at a place of pilgrimage, just as in our days multitudes of people travel together to Lourdes or Fatima. Why was this?

If we wish to know we have only to listen to what the people were saying. On all sides one heard the words, "A prophet! God has sent us a prophet."

You remember, do you not, the Prophets of the Old Testament: Elias, Isaias, Jeremias, Ezechiel, Daniel and many others? They played a great part in the history of Israel, for the word prophet means "one who speaks in the name of God." And these Prophets did in fact deliver God's message with remarkable courage, zeal and eloquence. When the chosen people, grown rich under the rule of their kings, turned away from God and ignored His commandments, it was the Prophets who dared to tell even the priests and the kings themselves that the day of punishment was coming. They said God would release the storm of His anger on the Promised Land and foretold the invasions of the Assyrians and the Babylonians who would capture Jerusalem and destroy it to its very foundations. As we know, everything happened exactly as the Prophets had foretold. But, when the time of trial came and the unhappy Israelites were deported to the banks of the Euphrates, it was these Prophets who kept the hopes of the people alive. They reminded them that their sufferings would cease when they had earned God's pardon, and that one day the chosen people would be free again and Jerusalem restored to its former greatness.

However, at the time of which we write, no prophet had raised his voice in Israel for five hundred years. In five long centuries, no one had arisen to remind the people of their Covenant with God. In all this time, while violence and injustice prevailed, there was no mighty voice to rebuke evil men for their crimes. We can easily understand, therefore, the emotion and excitement that filled men's hearts when the rumor spread like wildfire that at last a new prophet had appeared. After all this time, was God about to speak to His people?

"Yes, yes," the people said to one another, "a prophet has come to us, a true prophet, just like those we read of in the Scriptures. Who knows, perhaps it may even be Elias who did not die but who was long ago taken by God to heaven. How well this newcomer speaks! His words are like the crack of a whip, so that whoever hears them feels the guilt of his sins and longs for the forgiveness of God. . . . Wonderful events are taking place not far from the Dead Sea; near Bethany."

This was the reason why long lines of men and women filled the roads of Palestine, all making their way to the ford on the Jordan. They hoped to hear divine truths and to see with their own eyes one who spoke for the Most High.

Now the man whose burning words were drawing such crowds was none other than the son of Mary's cousin Elizabeth. His birth, as we already know, was the result of a miracle; it seemed as though God had caused this child to be born especially for His service and had a very definite plan for him to carry out. The child's parents were well aware of this. At his birth, they had consecrated him to the Lord; thenceforth he would serve God alone and would have no other task in life but to carry out the divine Will. As was the custom in Israel in such cases, he never shaved or cut his hair, after the manner of that other great servant of God, Samson.

Let us try to picture for ourselves this child now grown to manhood, heavily bearded, hairy, with burning eyes, yellow complexion and wasted body. As was the custom among the Prophets of old, his clothing was the skins of wild animals, fastened around his waist by a leather belt. For years now he had lived alone on the fringe of the desert, without a roof over his head or bed or furniture of any kind, sleeping all the year round under the open skies. For food he depended on what he could find in the desert: berries, wild honey and those yellow and black locusts which to this day the Arabs like to munch after the insects have been dried in the sun. (If you think this diet a strange one, think of the queer food people eat even in these days, such as frogs and snails.) The prophet preached repentance and self-denial to the people and, as we see, he practiced what he preached.

This strange man, this prophet, was called John, which in Hebrew means "God is kind," a name given to him at birth by his father on God's command. We always refer to him as John the Baptist in order to distinguish him from that other John, the Evangelist, who wrote the last of the four Gospels. He was given the name of "the Baptist" while he was actually preaching on the banks of the Jordan and here is the reason:

To all who came to listen to him, John unceasingly preached the need of repentance. Again and again he told the people, "Do penance for your sins and ask pardon for them. If you crave God's mercy, cleanse yourselves from your sins. If you are unhappy, it is because you have sinned." Then, when a man or woman among his hearers declared that he wished to renounce his sins and to lead a better life, John performed a ceremony which he called "baptism" to mark the great change in him. The penitent waded into the waters of the Jordan and prayed God for forgiveness while John pronounced a few words over him. Just as the body is cleansed by water so does God cleanse the soul from sin. The penitent emerged from the ceremony resolved to lead a better life. That is why so many people came to kneel before John, and entered the waters of the Jordan hoping that God would pardon them.

In addition to urging the people to repentance, John had another message, one that was listened to by the men of his day with deep emotion. He told his listeners that very soon there would appear another personage infinitely greater and holier than himself. "I am," he said, "the voice of one crying in the wilderness: make straight the way of the Lord." At other times, foretelling the future as did the Prophets of old, he would cry, "He is coming, one mightier than I, the latchet of whose shoes I am unworthy to untie. And when he comes, he will take a fan and will separate the wheat from the chaff. He will gather the good wheat into his barn, but the chaff he will burn with eternal fire."

When they heard this the people asked each other, "Who is this new messenger of whom he speaks? Surely it must be the Messias Himself whose coming the Prophets foretold so many centuries ago.

What will happen when He appears among us?" And there mounted
in them all a great uneasiness, a mixture of hope and of fear.

Now, in the early days of the year A.D. 28, there appeared in
the crowd surrounding John the Baptist a man from Galilee, in
appearance no different from many others. In the crowd there were
many Galileans, and they could be known by their accent, for it was
different from that of the people of Judea. This man was by trade a
woodworker, a journeyman carpenter, but this did not distinguish
Him in any particular way, for in the Palestine of that day carpentry was a common trade. This man was just over thirty years of age
and called Himself Jesus.

The moment, however, that the newcomer approached him,
John was overwhelmed. For God inspired his soul and he knew who
his visitor was, so that he, the prophet, trembled. This was no ordinary mortal, but the Almighty God, the very soul of purity. Why
was He, who had never been touched by the stain of sin, standing
among these sinners who had come to do penance? John recognized
the Son of God and murmured to Him, "I ought to be baptized by
Thee, and comest Thou to me?"

We can well understand John's surprise, for what need had
Jesus of the baptism of penance? Jesus acted as He did for one reason only: to teach men the necessity of baptism and to set them an
example. That is why in our own times we baptize new-born children (although we no longer dip them in a river but pour water
over their heads), so that the holy water will efface the stain of original sin. That is why at baptism the child's godparents promise in
its name that it will live in purity and according to God's law. Jesus
said to John, "Do as I say; for we must fulfill what the Father has
decreed."

And now a wonderful event took place which was later related
by John the Baptist himself. John did as Jesus bade him, and went
on with the baptism. As Jesus stood in the water praying, John
raised his eyes to heaven to call on the name of the Lord and he

saw the Holy Ghost descending from the blue vault of heaven in the form of a dove. It flew above them in the air above Jesus' head. The Baptist was but a man, and we can imagine his emotion when God thus proclaimed His envoy, His messenger, His own Son. It was a glorious and miraculous moment. And as his heart beat madly in his breast, John heard a voice from heaven saying, "This is my beloved Son, in whom I am well pleased."

The Gospels do not tell us whether this event took place in full view of the crowd. Did other eyes than those of the prophet watch the descent from heaven of the Holy Ghost in the form of a dove? Did any ears but his hear the voice of the Most High? We do know that John made no secret of the revelation made to him, and indeed why should he? Instead, he told everything he had seen and heard to a selected few among the crowd, those who seemed to him the wisest and best among them.

It is hard for us to realize the impression made by John's words on those who heard them. As soon as he told the story, it flew from mouth to mouth. "Yes, the Saviour who was promised to us is alive on earth. He was right here on the banks of the Jordan only a few minutes ago. He looked just like the rest of us, but it was really and truly He—He, the Messias for whose coming we have waited so long." In his Gospel, St. John the Evangelist writes so beautifully of these events, and tells the story so well, that we can almost see the people, wild with joy, running to tell the glorious news to their friends and relatives. And truly this was an event to make men weep for joy.

V

The Awaited Messias

THE MESSIAS! Do you know what the word meant to a Jew of the period when Jesus lived? Do you know why John the Baptist was so overwhelmed when he knew who it was that stood before him? And why the people wept and embraced one another for joy when they heard the news?

Let us go back two thousand years into history, two thousand years before the birth of Christ. This takes us to the beginning of a wonderful story that was to end only with the coming of Jesus. At that time a very small nation received a message from God. God said to its leader Abraham, "Because you believe in Me and do not worship idols as other peoples do, I shall protect you and there shall be a Covenant between us. You shall be My witnesses on earth, and you shall teach men the religion of the One True God. And in return I will make you My chosen people, a people privileged above all others, and I will give you My special protection."

God kept His promise down through the centuries and gave visible protection to His people. He led them first in Abraham's time from Mesopotamia to Palestine, the Promised Land. Here He allowed them to settle, and He proved by numerous miracles that He was constantly watching over them and helping them. Six or seven centuries later when the Israelites—for that was the name of this people—had been forced by famine to take refuge in Egypt and were being persecuted by a cruel Pharaoh, it was once more God who sent Moses to free them.

Of course, God's special protection was given to the people only if they kept their promise; that is, if they did not worship false gods and strictly obeyed the Commandments given to Moses on

Mount Sinai. Men, however, are only human. It happens from time to time that, even realizing they should love God, they disobey Him and break His laws. So it was on several occasions with the people of Israel. Some of them turned to such pagan idols, others fell into every form of wickedness. Finally, God grew angry and decided to punish these people who broke His Covenant with them.

So there came upon the people the disasters that had been foretold by the Prophets. First came the fierce Mesopotamian invasions and the horrible persecutions which followed: then the long and sorrowful exile in Babylon, far from their beloved home in Palestine. Suffering, however, brings man closer to God. At last the Israelites understood that they had sinned; they repented and prayed God to forgive them. Forthwith, as the Prophets had foretold, God's anger ceased. The Persian King Cyrus conquered Mesopotamia, and God inspired him to allow the chosen people to return to Palestine. This came about some five hundred years before Jesus came on earth. The Babylonian exile ended and the Israelites—now called the Jews—returned to their own country, having learned the terrible lesson inflicted on them by God. From now on, their one desire would be to serve Him.

After the return from the Babylonian exile in the fifth century B.C., Palestine was no more than a province belonging to one of the vast empires that in turn ruled the Eastern world. First it formed part of the mighty Persian Empire, being governed by a "satrap," an official of the Persian Emperor known as "the King of Kings." Then, at the end of the fourth century B.C., when Alexander the Great of Greece had conquered the Persians, it became a Greek province. Finally, when the Roman power covered all the Mediterranean basin, the Holy Land became part of the Roman Empire. This was in the year 67 B.C., when Jerusalem was captured. From that time on, on the streets, on the walls, and in the fortresses of Palestine, the Roman legionnaires, clad in crimson and with heavy shoes and long pikes, stood on guard.

So it was that for five hundred years, apart from a few brief in-terruptions, Palestine had lain under the heel of a conqueror. This was an unhappy situation and it left her people restless and fearful. The conquerors might change, but the result for the people was much the same. At the time of Jesus' birth, the Romans, as we have seen, had made the tyrant Herod governor of Palestine. Later on, at the time of Jesus' baptism, Herod was dead and the Romans al-lowed his son, Herod Antipas, to rule only the north of Palestine. They had installed an official of their own, Pontius Pilate, as "proc-urator" or governor, of Jerusalem. But whoever the ruler of the moment or place might be, the Jews were oppressed and discon-tented. Quite naturally, they longed for their lost freedom and prayed to God to restore it to them.

You can be very sure that at this period in their history the Jews had learned to turn to God for help. Indeed, it must be said to their credit that during these five centuries they had defended their religion with passionate fervor against all pagan attacks. Neither by force nor persuasion could the Greeks or Romans entice the Jews away from their worship of the One True God. In their sad state of semi-slavery, these Jews, these descendants of the Temple of the Covenant, knew that in God and God alone lay their hope and their protection. The words of their Kings, the history of their race, the magnificent Psalms of King David and the other great Hebrew poets had by now all been written down in the book we call the Bible. This book the Jews studied unceasingly.

So it was that in this tiny country of Palestine, among this people of less than a million souls, history's greatest lesson of all was a living reality. Israel had preserved her faith in God. Great events might take place in the outside world, new cities might arise, great literature be written or great battles be fought—to the true Jew all this meant little. When in the year 14 (after Christ's birth) Augustus died and Tiberius succeeded him as Roman emperor, the people of Jerusalem paid hardly any attention. What really mattered to them was the Law of God, and the daily morning and evening prayers for which they gathered in the courtyard of the Temple, their faces turned toward the Holy of Holies. One question above all lay deep in the heart of every Jew: when would the Lord take pity on His people and finally forgive them their sins? Would God restore to them their past glory and their proud independence? When would the era of liberty dawn for Israel?

Now, for many long centuries in Israel's history those spokesmen of God who were called Prophets had foretold that the day of freedom and happiness would certainly come, with the help of an all-powerful and supernatural leader who would be sent them expressly by God. As far back as the days of the Patriarchs, Jacob on his deathbed had seen this figure shining through the mists of the future. In many of his Psalms, King David had sung the glory of His coming. All the great Prophets, Isaias, Ezechiel and Daniel among them, had foretold with absolute certainty of the coming of the Saviour.

This messenger of liberty and justice was called by the somewhat vague name we have mentioned, "the anointed of God," or in Hebrew, the "Messias." The Greeks translated this term as "Christos, or Christ." Consequently, for a Jew of this period, the coming of the Messias meant the wonderful moment when the people of Israel would be restored to the full friendship of God, when God's final pardon would be granted to them, when their past glories would be revived.

It was no wonder then that people talked and talked with each other about the coming of the Messias. They wondered what He would be like. They studied the smallest references to Him in the sayings of the Prophets, in the hope of finding some clue. In certain texts of the Bible, the Messias was referred to as the "Son of God," but, on the other hand, the prophet Daniel called Him the "Son of Man." What did that mean? Was He going to be God and man at the same time? Could He be mortal like other men and immortal like the Eternal God Himself? It did not seem very clear, and there were endless arguments about the matter.

There was still more discussion about the manner in which the Messias would carry out His mission. Some declared that He would come as a mighty king, more powerful than any of the rulers of the earth, and that He would use the forces at His command to defeat and wipe out forever the enemies of Israel. This idea of the Messias was a natural one among a people who had been enslaved for five hundred years and who had one desire: to take vengeance on their oppressors.

Others, however, who had studied other less numerous but very beautiful and moving passages from the Bible, were convinced that the Messias would not come to take vengeance on anyone; that His message would be only one of love, justice and mercy. In the prophecies of Isaias there was even one beautiful text which described the Messias as a man in appearance like other men; He would suffer on earth as all humans do and His sufferings would redeem the sins of men and obtain for them the forgiveness of God.

Whatever opinion men held in these discussions one thing is certain: that every believing Jew longed for the coming of the Messias. You remember how, in the Temple, the saintly old Simeon gave thanks to God for having allowed him to live to see the day of His coming. When people asked John the Baptist, as they often did, if he himself was the Messias, John replied, "No, I am not He. But He will surely come soon." And it was generally believed in Israel at that period that the time of His coming was at hand. In a text by the prophet Daniel there appeared a mysterious phrase which said that he would come in "seventy weeks of years," which meant 490 years, or roughly five centuries. Now, just that period had passed since these words were written and so . . .

Now you can see why it was that the humblest Jew trembled with joy when he heard it said, "Haven't you heard? The Messias has been born, He is here amongst us. People have seen Him, and soon He will show Himself and begin His reign on earth." At the beginning of the Gospel of St. John we find a magnificently poetic passage recalling the feverish hope with which people awaited "the true Light, that enlightens every man who comes into the world." The events that took place at the ford of Bethany, the vision that John the Baptist had seen and revealed to others, were proof of the matter. The Light of the world had come to earth and from now on it would shine brightly.

VI

Jesus Reveals Himself
as the Messias

THE SCENE OF OUR STORY now moves to the desert, to a vast jumble of rocks on the slope of a steep mountain. Above them, near the top of the mountain, there are natural caves in the cliffs which overlook a great stretch of countryside, beautiful in spots but for the most part desolate. Through the expanse of yellow desert sand the river Jordan winds like a silver thread between two ribbons of fertile green while, in the far distance, rise rank upon rank of sun-scorched, dun-colored and barren hills and mountains. To the right, toward the south, the Dead Sea, surrounded by glittering salt marshes, sleeps in its canyon. It is a forbidding and deserted scene, but if we look closely we may see a man kneeling in silent prayer on the threshold of one of the caves. Don't you recognize Him? It is Jesus. We last saw Him after His baptism on the banks of the Jordan. What can He be doing out here in the desert?

As you grow older, you will learn from your own experience that before anyone starts on any great undertaking he will, if he is wise, reflect deeply and pray earnestly to God for good counsel and guidance. Such preparation was of course not necessary for Jesus, who was God Himself; but we may be sure that He undertook it in order to teach us an important lesson, while at the same time escaping from the world so that He could better converse with His Father in heaven.

For forty days He remained in His retreat praying and fasting, that is, taking no food of any kind. It was a terrible ordeal of hunger and thirst, endured in solitude under the burning heat. From time to time, He was buffeted by the winds and those terrible dark sand-storms of the desert. And, as the wind howled around Him, He heard the evil voice of the Devil, the enemy of God, the dark angel who long ago was cast into hell for his rebellion and who ever since labors unceasingly to oppose the will of God.

Toward the end of the forty days, hoping to take advantage of the fact that Jesus was weak from hunger, the tempter approached Him, saying, "If you are truly the Son of God, command that these stones be made into bread." It is easy to understand why the Devil spoke in this manner: first of all he wanted to find out if this Man was also God; and secondly, if Jesus accepted the challenge and per-formed a miracle, it would have seemed as though He acknowledged that He were the lesser of the two. But Satan this time had met One who was more than his match. Jesus replied with a simple quotation from the Bible, "Not by bread alone does man live, but by every word that comes from the mouth of God."

Now the tempter changed his tactics. He pointed out to Jesus the immense expanses of the earth stretching out before Him into the limitless spaces of Asia, and said to Him, "You see all the king-doms of the world? They belong to me, and I will give them to You if You will fall down and adore me." The Devil was not far wrong in his claim, for all too often worldly power and glory are gained by evil deeds, by violence and treachery. But it is hard to understand how he could expect Jesus to accept so absurd a proposal. In reply to him, the Messias simply quoted the first Commandment, "The Lord thy God thou shalt adore, and Him only shalt thou serve."

Baffled and furious, the tempter tried again. He carried Jesus to the pinnacle of the Temple in Jerusalem which from a dizzy height overlooked a deep ravine. "If you are truly the Son of God," the Devil said, "cast yourself down, for does not the Bible tell us that angels shall bear up the Son of God?" Of course, had Jesus wanted it, He could have been borne up by angels. But again, to summon them would be to perform a miracle at Satan's bidding. And we must remember that not once in the whole story of His life will we read of Christ working a miracle for His own benefit, to provide food for Himself, for example, or to escape from danger. This third attempt of the Devil was even more ridiculous than the two previous ones, and once again Jesus replied with a quotation from the Bible, "Thou shalt not tempt the Lord thy God." The meaning of this is that we should know that God will not work vain or foolish miracles.

Now the Devil acknowledged defeat and departed amid the howling of the tempest. A great calm fell, and angels appeared to serve Jesus and bring food to Him.

Early in the month of March, in A.D. 28, Jesus came down from the mountain. From that time began His public life which was to last for some two years. Yes, in no more than two short years we shall see unrolled the whole Gospel story. We shall hear the wonderful teachings and sayings of Christ, and see the foundation of that organization created by the Messias to carry on His work and which we call "the Church." It is hard to realize the unbelievable activity of Christ in accomplishing such an immense task in so short a time.

For two years He was ceaselessly on the move, preaching His message on all occasions, always ready to answer questions, welcoming all people and infinitely generous to all. Most of the time during the first year He was to be found in His native province of Galilee (see map at front of book) among the peasants and lake fishermen He knew so well. Later on, toward the end of His life, He was mostly in southern Palestine, in Judea, a less fertile land than Galilee where the people are more dour. In this province is located the capital city of Jerusalem. But Jesus made many journeys elsewhere, sometimes even beyond the frontiers of the Holy Land. He kept moving around all the time: visiting the Temple for the great religious festivals, by-passing districts which He deemed had already heard enough, or simply going to some place where help was needed or a good deed to be done.

In order to spread His teaching and deliver His message, Jesus relied first of all on the spoken word. Even today the Eastern peoples love to gather to listen to a public speaker. In Syria and Palestine it is not at all unusual to find groups of people sitting on the ground around an open air orator and listening to him with rapt attention. We should picture Jesus and His listeners in this setting. In those days there were, of course, no school buildings to which people went regularly for instruction, so we sometimes find Christ preaching in a synagogue, which was, as we know, a place for meeting and prayer. A synagogue was to be found in even the smallest Jewish hamlet, and in it every believing Jew had the right to express himself. Jesus used to claim this right and, reading a text from the Bible, He would then explain it perfectly. Sometimes, when He found Himself on the shores of Lake Tiberias, so beautiful with its clear waters and background of gentle hills, He would enter a boat, and, standing in the stern, preach to the multitude of listeners on the shore. On yet other occasions, when the crowd was very great, He would lead His congregation to some sloping hillside and there address them under the open sky.

When Jesus spoke, His words were wondrous to listen to. Everything He said was so simple and clear that it could be understood by everyone, but at the same time it was full of poetry that went to the very hearts of His listeners. The phrases He used could come only from Him; sometimes grave and even severe, sometimes gentle and touched with humor. Even today, when we read them in the Gospel, many of them strike us with overwhelming force. Imagine then how they must have impressed the people who heard them from His own lips.

But it was not only through His sermons that Christ made known His message, for everything served as an occasion to advise and teach His followers. Very often one simple sentence or brief remark was all that He needed to make clear to everyone the truths of religion, the true teachings of God. And throughout His life Christ taught as much by example as He did by words. His smallest act was perfect, and not once in anything He said or did can we find the smallest trace of ill-will, untruthfulness or violence— nothing but goodness, absolute sincerity and calm firmness. Can you wonder then that such a man drew people to Him, or that in such a little time He was able to complete a work that will last for all eternity?

You may perhaps wonder why, since Jesus was God Himself and therefore all-powerful, He did not reveal His message like a thunderclap in one terrifying display of His power. Why did He not wish to appear in the Temple at Jerusalem arrayed as a mighty king and surrounded by hosts of angels? He could, of course, have done so, and if He had, all the peoples of the world would have bowed before Him and believed in Him. But even if they did, would it all have meant very much? Would people who believed merely because they had seen impressive happenings have been changed for the better? Would they have renounced their sins, or would they truly have understood Christ's teaching? Not a bit of it. And so Jesus acted in quite a different manner. By the way He chose to perform His mission He teaches us that an important task can be worked out only with wisdom and patience and that it must be quietly begun.

In the beginning of His public life, He revealed the truth about Himself gradually. He did nothing spectacular, such as proclaiming before the rulers of Israel that He was the Messias. On the contrary, He gave His message first to humble folk, people of no particular importance. Above all, Jesus seeks those of simple faith who are ready to receive Him.

Let us watch Him, for example, at a wedding feast in a little Galilean village called Cana. He was the guest of a family of simple peasants who had done their best to arrange this little celebration in honor of their daughter's wedding. As with countryfolk everywhere, a wedding gave an opportunity for simple gaiety and a good meal. But on this occasion, after some hours the supply of wine ran out. It may have been that the bride's father had not the money to buy much wine, but in any case he was very embarrassed and distressed. Mary, Jesus' mother, noticed her host's plight and, feeling very sorry for these good people, she approached her Son and whispered to Him, "They have no more wine." We can but be touched at the utter confidence in her Son which Mary displayed by these simple words. The Blessed Virgin knew that He was all-powerful; she had known it ever since the Angel Gabriel had spoken to her thirty years before. She knew that now He had only to say the word for the world's best wine to appear on the table. What was Jesus going to do? Would He yield to His Mother's request? It might seem strange that He should work a miracle merely to provide wine for a gathering of peasants. And yet, He did just that. He gave orders for the empty wine jars, of the kind found in every Jewish household of the period, to be filled with water. This was done, and instantly the water was changed into delicious wine. Mary's prayer was granted, as will be the prayers of everyone who appeals to Jesus with absolute faith and sincerity. So it was that these humble Galilean peasants were among the first to learn that this man like themselves, a simple fellow guest, possessed powers so extraordinary that they could belong only to God.

Here is another equally charming story. One day Jesus was making His way back from Jerusalem to Galilee, following the mountain road that crosses the province of Samaria. We must tell you that at this time relations were not too good between the Samaritans and the Jews; there were frequent quarrels between them, and the faithful of Judea looked upon the Samaritans as heretics and unclean. Now, during the journey, Jesus felt thirsty and halted at a well; here He sat down, for He had no vessel so that He could draw the water for Himself. Presently there came down from the village a woman carrying her water pitcher on her head, as was the custom of the country.

Jesus said to her, "Give me to drink."

In great surprise, the woman said to Him, "How do you, a Jew, ask a drink of me, who am a Samaritan?"

We, of course, know why Jesus acted thus: to show that in His eyes all these old quarrels were finished and that His goodness and love extended to all. He replied to the woman with the somewhat puzzling phrase, "If you knew who I am, it is of Me that you would ask for water, and the water I would give you would be living water."

At first, of course, the woman did not understand Him. She did not realize that the living water of which Jesus spoke was the Word of God which ever comes to refresh our souls and to appease our thirst. Jesus then explained, and at once this humble woman was overwhelmed.

"Sir," she cried, "give me this water. . . ." She spoke so simply and with such ardent faith that the heart of Jesus was moved. He

spoke to her, and it was to this humble stranger of an outcast race that He revealed the full truth: that He was the Messias, the bearer of the Good News, the Giver of the living water of faith. Here again we see that Jesus revealed Himself not to the rich and powerful, but to a poor humble woman who believed in Him.

Jesus asked nothing more than complete faith in Him from those who wished to follow Him. Here is yet another story, this time of an officer in the Roman army, whose prayer was instantly granted because of his faith. This centurion—we would call him a captain—lived in a little town on the shores of Lake Tiberias, called Capharnaum. He had already heard of Jesus and of the astonishing things that were told about Him. He had in his house a servant to whom he was deeply attached and who had fallen seriously ill. Learning that Jesus was in the neighborhood, he sent a messenger to Him, begging Him to cure the sick man. Jesus at once set out for the centurion's house, and was met on the way by a second message: "Lord, I am not worthy that thou shouldst enter under my roof: but only say the word, and my servant shall be healed."

Here is a faith that we can well admire. Faith and humility were what Jesus most loved in men. He was deeply moved and cried out, "Amen, I say to you, I have not found such faith in Israel." This centurion was not even a Jew: it is probable he was a pagan, yet Jesus did not hesitate for an instant in granting his prayer. He spoke the word He had been asked to speak. And when the messengers returned to their master, they learned that the sick servant had been cured at the exact moment when Jesus spoke.

There are many other stories such as these in the Gospel. From the three you have just read you must remember this important lesson: Jesus did not appear suddenly in splendor to reveal His heavenly mission to the rich and powerful of the world. Instead, He chose to do so simply, gradually and quietly, to humble people of simple faith.

^^

VII

The Twelve Apostles

EVERY GREAT LEADER or personage needs, as you know, a certain number of men to help him in his task, to carry out his orders, and, if need be, to continue his work should he become unable to do so. Jesus was far greater than any leader or king, but as it was His will that while on earth He should act as a man, He decided to choose helpers or disciples to labor with Him in the spreading of the Good News. The twelve men He chose were called APOSTLES and they played a very important part in His plan of action.

How did He choose them? Here we see the strange charm for souls, the shining attraction of the personality of Jesus. Already, at the ford of Bethany, three of John the Baptist's friends were won over by Him the moment they met Him, and there and then they decided to leave everything and follow Him. These three—Andrew, John and Simon—became the first of Jesus' disciples. Some little time later, in the course of one of His journeys, Christ found a fourth; Jesus, who could read the most secret thoughts of man, gazed long on this man and knew that he was worthy of the task to which he was about to be called. Jesus simply said, "Follow Me." Instantly Philip obeyed and went with Him without discussion. On yet another occasion the call came to a minor government official, a collector of taxes named Matthew. Jesus bade him to leave his table and his monies and his accounts and said, "Follow Me." And Matthew, too, answered the divine call and left everything to follow his Master down the road. It was Matthew who was to become the first of the Evangelists.

What extraordinary power did Jesus have that immediately in-

spired everyone to want to serve Him? We now come to the most remarkable scene of all those in which He chose His followers. Try to
picture for yourself a fine morning just before sunrise on the shores
of Lake Tiberias. The water has the milky color of pearl, the shore is
shaded in brown and mauve, and the sun is just about to rise behind
the dark blue mountains of Galaad. A party of men are returning
from their night's fishing in one of those large boats such as are still
in use on the lake and which can hold a dozen fishermen. The men
are tired and dispirited, for they have been out all night and have
caught nothing.

As they pull into the bank, they see Jesus who leaps on board.
"Launch out into the deep, and let down your nets," He tells them.
The men hesitate, for it seems useless to do so. "Master, we have
labored all the night and have taken nothing," they said. But in
spite of this they have such faith in Jesus that they do as He bids
them. At once a miracle takes place. Scarcely have the nets been
cast than they tighten and stretch. Through the ropes that hold
them the fishermen can feel the fish jumping. The catch is so heavy
that the men are unable to handle it and have to call on the crew of
a neighboring boat for help. Even so, the two boats are almost
swamped under the weight of this enormous catch. At once these
simple men realize that it is not merely to provide them with fish
that Jesus has worked this miracle and that it has a particular
meaning for them. They kneel before Him, ready to follow Him
and obey His commands.

"Fear not," the Master tells them, "from henceforth you shall
catch men." He had perceived in this boat's crew of honest workers the men best suited to help in His great mission. For their part,
they understood and answered His call and, leaving their boat,
their nets and their fish, they followed Him, filled with joy at having been chosen.

You now see who were these twelve men chosen by Jesus to
help Him in His task. They were neither rich nor powerful nor

well-educated. On the contrary, they were humble Galilean farmers or lake fishermen or small businessmen. But Jesus chose them because He saw in them the qualities needed for the work He intended to do: unquestioning faith in Him, high courage, and a spirit of sacrifice sufficient to make them accept the hard and dangerous life that would be theirs from now on.

For, as you can well imagine, life with Jesus was not going to be easy and comfortable. He had warned His disciples that in His service they would have to give up all their worldly possessions. They would have to say good-by to their families, even their parents. They must abandon their trades, relying for their needs on Providence, on the gifts and alms they would receive. For clothing they would have only the barest necessities, a cloak and sandals, and a staff for their journeys. In their hearts there would be room for nothing but Christ's message, the Good News that it would be their duty to carry to all parts of the world.

All this the disciples accepted joyfully. We must have a deep admiration for these first followers of Christ, these fathers of Christianity, who simply because they believed in Jesus, sacrificed for Him everything that makes life easy. And, from the very beginning, they were ready to lay down their lives for Him.

The disciples were of all ages. Simon, we know, was a fully matured man, an employer of other fishermen, with a comfortable position in life. John was a very young man, hardly more than a boy, and for this reason Jesus always showed a particular tenderness toward him, so much so that he is often called "the beloved disciple."

The Apostles differed as much in character as they did in age. Simon was an enthusiast, full of eager faith, generous and fiery. John was above all a youth of keen intellect, who listened even more carefully than the others to every word of the Master and was quicker than they to pick up His meaning. Then there was Thomas, a cautious man, who needed proof before he believed, but whose belief, once he was convinced, withstood all trials. Philip, the worthy Philip, was simple and friendly, always ready to give himself wholeheartedly to his work. At heart, this little group of twelve men were very human. They had their virtues and their weaknesses like all of us, but Jesus' love was to transform them, simple as they were, into great saints.

And now, how did Christ make use of their services? Well, He employed them on any and every task that falls to the lot of the immediate assistants of any great leader or missionary. When they planned a journey to a strange district, two of the Twelve went on in advance to secure a lodging for the party and to find out how best to assemble the people to hear Jesus. When great crowds gathered to listen to Him, it was the Twelve who directed the congregation and seated them, maintained order and sometimes even provided food for the multitude. In Christ's absence, one or another of them took His place, and sometimes He sent them in pairs to preach His mission in places chosen by Him, to speak in His name and even to perform miracles on His behalf. (Indeed, the exact meaning of the word "Apostle" is "Envoy.") How wonderfully fortunate were these disciples, and what a privilege it was for them to have been chosen by Jesus and called to labor at His side.

They were even more highly privileged than you think. For it was to them, His chosen friends, that Jesus revealed the truth of His divinity in a very special way. It was quite natural and understandable that He should explain matters more fully to those who worked directly with Him; that He should make it crystal clear to them that He was more than a great preacher or even a prophet; that He was, in fact, the Son of God.

You will remember the scene described in our first chapter when Jesus calmed the storm and so gave full proof of His power. There came another rather similar occasion, this time at night, when the Apostles were in a boat on Lake Tiberias. As they were making for the shore, a violent gale sprang up and drove them back into the open waters. But this time Jesus was not in the boat with them. At about three o'clock in the morning, when their arms were so tired with rowing that they could struggle no more and they began to despair of ever reaching port, suddenly they saw a white form approaching them, walking on the waters. They were terrified at the sight of what they thought to be a ghost and cried out in fear. Then a voice they knew well spoke to them across the storm-tossed waves, "It is I; be not afraid." The features of the apparition were not recognizable in the dark, so one of the Apostles cried out, "If it is really You, Lord, bid me too to walk upon the waters." "Come," called Jesus. The disciple jumped from the boat, but feeling the water move under his feet he began to doubt, and at once commenced to sink. But Jesus took him by the hand and helped him back into the boat. Here indeed was proof enough for the Apostles of the divine power of the Master; and what a lesson it teaches us of the necessity for absolute faith in Him!

On another occasion Jesus gave a still more dazzling proof of His divinity. It happened in the month of August in A.D. 29, during one of those blazing Eastern summers. Jesus took with Him three of His disciples, Simon, James and John, and led them to the top of a very high mountain. It was probably Mount Hermon, in the extreme north of Palestine, which rises some 8,800 feet in the clear air, its slopes covered with noble forests and its peak snow-clad for most of the year. They reached the summit, and all four were praying when suddenly the three Apostles were spellbound by an amazing sight. Before their eyes Jesus was transfigured. His features took on a majesty that was not of this earth, and His garments became shining and white as snow. On either side of Him appeared two figures whom the Apostles recognized: they were the great Moses and the prophet Elias carried up to Heaven by God so many centuries before. At the same time a voice spoke from the cloud which surrounded the three figures, saying, "This is my beloved Son; hear Him." In this scene of the "Transfiguration" what was revealed to the three favored Apostles was the indescribable glory and majesty of God.

It is not hard to understand why the Apostles followed Jesus with complete confidence, after being given such proofs of His divinity. This does not mean, however, that they understood His plans fully or at once. When Jesus showed them that He was truly the Son of God, all-powerful with the Father, they were joyful and filled with enthusiasm. But He often told them other things that disturbed them and almost made them doubt Him. He announced to them that one day He would go to Jerusalem, be arrested, tortured and finally put to death by His enemies, and that on the third day after His death He would rise again. To the Apostles all this seemed so strange as to be almost unbelievable. They knew, of course, that all things were possible to God, and therefore to Jesus; but why, they asked, should He, the Almighty One, accept suffering, torture and death? These Apostles were, as you see, only men, simple human beings. It was only much later, only after Christ's death and resurrection, that they were to understand everything.

Having thus chosen His Apostles and trained them for their task, it still remained for Jesus to appoint a leader among them. The more you see of life the more you will realize that no human association, whether it be a nation, or a regiment in the army, or, for that matter, a class in school, can work successfully without a leader. There must be one whose authority everybody accepts and who can unite the efforts of all for the welfare of all. Jesus, therefore, decided to appoint a leader of the Apostles, and this is how He set about it.

During a journey He made with the Apostles to the district of Caesarea Philippi (see front map, toward the top) the group halted one day near the springs at the mouth of the River Jordan, and Jesus asked them, "Who do men say that I am?" With that, most of the Apostles repeated various opinions they had heard. "Some say John the Baptist; and some Elias, and others Jeremias or one of the other prophets." All these answers proved that most people still did not understand who Jesus really was.

"But who do you say that I am?" said Jesus. At this, Simon, the fervent and generous Simon, the captain of the crew that had

caught the miraculous draught of fishes, cried out without a moment's hesitation, "Thou art Christ, the Son of the Living God." Simon had understood Jesus perfectly. His trust in Him was so great that the whole truth had been made plain to him.

"Blessed are you, Simon," said Jesus. "No man has revealed this to you, but My Father who is in heaven. And now I say to thee: You have been called Simon, but now you are Peter, and upon this rock I will build my Church. And I will give to you the keys of the

Kingdom of heaven, and God will receive those to whom you open the gates. The man whose sins you shall forgive, I also will forgive him!" And, turning toward the others, he told them that Peter was their leader. This is why, down all the long centuries, the Church—that is, all those who are faithful to the true teachings of Christ—has always recognized as its leaders those men who one after another in an unbroken line have succeeded Peter. These are the Popes, the men whose faith has never failed; through them the Spirit of God still speaks to man.

VIII

How Jesus Spoke to the People

FROM NOW on the news ran like wildfire throughout the villages and along the roads of Palestine.

"Haven't you heard of the new prophet who has appeared?" travelers would ask.

"Why? Is He then greater than John the Baptist from Jordan's banks?"

"Greater! He is a hundred times, a thousand times greater; if you only could hear Him speak, or see the miracles He performs, you would know how great He is! . . . Some people think He is the Messias Himself."

"The Messias! If that is so, let us hasten to throw ourselves at His feet!"

And so hordes of people, crowds even bigger than those that followed John the Baptist, made their way to the hills of Galilee to see and hear for themselves this Man who, some said, might prove to be the very Messias Himself.

Let us try to picture for ourselves these people who made such haste to answer the call of Jesus. Some, no doubt, were merely curious; anxious to see for themselves this Man of whom everybody was talking. But there were others, many others, who were filled with faith and good will. With all their hearts they hoped that the rumor was true and that the true Messias had at last appeared on earth. Among the crowds were many Galileans, honest farmers and fishermen from the surrounding districts; others came from farther afield, Judeans still covered with the dust of their long journey.

Jesus' fame had spread even beyond the frontiers of Palestine and so there were groups of Jews from the Phenician cities of Tyre and Sidon who had taken up the pilgrims' staff and knapsack to come to Him. Some traveled by themselves, others in family groups, and among them were many invalids and cripples who hoped that the "Prophet" would cure them. None of them, of course, could have had the least idea of the unique opportunity they were to have of hearing God Himself speak to man through the mouth of Jesus. But it was a fine thing of them to travel so many weary miles and to endure such hardship. This is why Jesus, in His infinite goodness, spoke to them and taught them so tirelessly.

What a wonderful thing it would be for us if we, too, could listen to one of Jesus' sermons! What would we do if we were to learn suddenly that the Son of God was here; that His voice was to be heard in one of our city squares? Would we not be overcome by emotion and run with all our might to find Him? That cannot be but, by great good fortune, we can read one of His discourses almost exactly as it came from His lips. Two of the Evangelists, St. Matthew and St. Luke, have recorded it so faithfully that we can follow it almost as if Jesus Himself were speaking.

Try to imagine that we find ourselves among one of those crowds that pressed around the Messias more than nineteen hundred years ago. The crowd is so large that it has overflowed the synagogue and even the village square, and has followed Jesus to the slope of one of the high hills that overlook the Lake of Tiberias (that is why this particular discourse by Jesus is often called "The Sermon on the Mount"). The Apostles have arranged the huge crowd in orderly fashion, seating them in rows on the fresh green grass of springtime. Beneath their eyes they behold a panorama of rare beauty: the waters of the lake are blue and calm, reflecting in their depths the clouds above them, a long procession of flamingos flying overhead traces a pattern of pink against the heavens; and on the horizon Mount Hermon is lit by the rays of the rising sun. Suddenly a great silence falls over the multitude as Jesus rises up. Standing on an isolated rock, so that He is visible to all, He begins to speak:

"Blessed are the poor in spirit: for theirs is the kingdom of heaven."

"Blessed are they that hunger and thirst after justice: for they shall have their fill."

"Blessed are they that mourn: for they shall be comforted."

"Blessed are they that suffer persecution for justice sake: for theirs is the kingdom of heaven."

The voice of Jesus falls clearly on the still air, so that His listeners hear every word perfectly. But what do these strange words mean? Most people would say that there is little to rejoice about in

being poor, hungry, afflicted and persecuted. So, from His very first word, Jesus has caught the attention of His listeners and aroused their interest. We can be sure that among them are many poor people, even men and women so poor that they have not enough to eat, and to them Jesus seems to be saying, "Have confidence, for one day, when your life here is ended, you will find eternal happiness." Also present, we may be sure, are many who suffer either in body or spirit because of illness or because they mourn the loss of someone dear. To them, Jesus says, "Be of good hope, be brave, for the time will come when all your suffering will end, when you will once more be united to those you love." How beautiful and consoling are these little phrases with which our Lord begins His sermon, and because of them it is sometimes referred to as "the Sermon of the Beatitudes" (in Latin the word "happy" is *beatus*).

And now Jesus continues with His list of those who will find happiness in the kingdom of heaven: the meek, the merciful, the pure of heart, peace-lovers who wish no ill to anyone. To all of these He promises the reward that God has reserved for those He loves. And already, from His very first words, His listeners feel in themselves the rebirth of courage and zeal. They had been perhaps sad, uneasy in their minds, sick at heart, but these few words of His have consoled them.

Now Jesus changes the subject of His discourse. In Eastern countries, public speakers pay much less attention than we do to preparing a speech where each part follows a natural sequence as we are taught to do when writing a composition. There, speakers are much more concerned with impressing their audiences with imaginative phrases; they try to grip their hearers' attention with some expression that can be easily remembered. At first, this manner of speaking seems a bit confusing to our Western ears, but it needs only a second's thought for us to realize that Christ's slightest word has the deepest and richest of meanings.

Having thus aroused His listeners to a pitch of hope and fer-

vor that will remain with them for as long as He speaks to them,
Jesus now approaches a subject that they will find a bit more difficult to understand and to accept. The greater part of His listeners
are Jews who have been brought up in the religion of their ancestors, according to the laws which God gave to Moses on Mount
Sinai and which are explained in full detail in the Bible. We can be
quite sure that many of those present must have asked themselves
anxiously as they made their way to Him, "Does this Jesus, of whom
we have heard such wonderful stories, belong to our religion? Is He
faithful to the teachings of God which, since the time of Abraham,
have been revealed to us through the Patriarchs, through Moses
and through the Prophets? On the other hand, if He is only going
to explain the texts of the Bible, there is nothing very new or original about Him. And if this is all we are going to hear from Him,
it will hardly have been worth our while to come."

Jesus, of course, knew exactly what was passing through the
minds of His audience and so He declared to them, "Do not think
that I am come to destroy the law. . . . I am not come to destroy,
but to fulfill."

You may find this sentence a little difficult to understand, but
it is easy to explain just what Jesus meant by it. First of all, He
assures His listeners that, like them all, He is faithful to the truths
that God had revealed throughout the centuries to the Jewish
people and that are to be found enshrined in the Bible.

To set their minds completely at rest on this point, He continues, "Amen, I say to you that heaven and earth shall pass away,
but God's teaching shall not pass away. He who disobeys the Commandments of God shall not enter the Kingdom of heaven."

This, surely, is clear enough for anyone, but it does not mean
that the Son of God has come to earth merely to confirm the teachings of Moses and the Prophets. Just listen again, "I have not come
to destroy the Law . . . but to fulfill." By "fulfill," Jesus means to
complete the Law, by explaining its full meaning, which few had
understood up to this time. Next, Jesus explains exactly what He

means, "You have heard that it was said to them of old: 'Thou shalt not kill. Whoever kills shall be punished.' But I will go further than this: whoever is angry with his brother or insults him shall also be punished. If therefore, when you are about to offer a gift at the altar of God, you remember some quarrel or serious disagreement you have had with another, leave your offering and make your peace with him, for this is the way in which you shall best please God."

You see, of course, how much more the teachings of Jesus demand than did the Jewish Law. Jesus forbids not merely the crime of killing, but all violence and hatred. It is a difficult teaching to obey, but how beautiful it is! Continuing to give further examples to His listeners in order to impress upon them the importance of what He is saying, Jesus reminds them of the old proverb, "an eye for an eye, and a tooth for a tooth," which means that if you are wronged you can do a like wrong in return. This, He tells them, is a severe and brutal rule which must no longer be applied. They must forgive wrongs done to them and cease to seek revenge. They must do good to those that injure them. For is there any one of us who is not himself in need of forgiveness, who is not in need of God's mercy? God will forgive us just in so far as we forgive others.

Here is another example of how much the teaching of Jesus was in advance of Jewish Law: hitherto a man was allowed to have several wives, and we know that such great figures in the Bible as David and Solomon had very many indeed, and also that the Law permitted divorce. What did Jesus say? That a man could have only one wife, to be loved and cherished all his life long as the companion given him by God to be the mother of his children. Here indeed was a change for the better.

So the golden moments passed away as Jesus continued His sermon. No one could ever tire of listening to the divine voice which spoke words so beautiful and simple, words His listeners could later meditate on in solitude or discuss at length with their companions.

You yourselves have heard these great teachings of Christ almost from babyhood and, even if the time has not yet come for you to put them fully into practice, you still cannot ignore them. Every time, for instance, that you recite the Our Father you repeat Christ's words, "Forgive us our trespasses as we forgive those who trespass against us." Now just try to imagine the effect of this astonishingly new commandment on its hearers when it fell on their ears for the first time. "Love your enemies"—it was almost as though the world had turned upside down.

But at the same time He proclaimed these new lessons in such sublime terms, Jesus also gave simple and direct advice, the value of which everyone could test from his own experience.

When, for instance, He said, "How is it you can see the speck of dust in your brother's eye, and cannot see the beam in your own? Hypocrite! take the beam out of your own eye first, and then you can see how to take the speck from your brother's." You will, I am sure, understand what this means. It is of course that all of us are inclined to criticize other people and to find fault with them while completely overlooking our own much more serious defects. There is a very deep lesson for all of us in this simple comparison of the speck and the beam.

Here is another simple example in which Jesus makes His message clear: "There is no good tree that brings forth evil fruit; nor an evil tree that brings forth good fruit. Every tree is known by its fruit. Men do not gather grapes from thorns, or figs from thistles. . . ." Simple words, but with what a deep meaning! Beginning with ourselves, how many people do we not know who are full of fine words and who boast of putting Christ's teachings into practice but whose deeds are far from being always good. The good fruits of which Jesus speaks are good deeds, and it is by his actions that we know if a man is really good. "Why," asked Jesus again, "do you call Me, Lord, Lord, and still do not do the things that I say?" If we really wish to please God, He told us we must not be content with words, but live holy, just and virtuous lives.

Here is yet another very useful piece of advice given by Jesus in the Sermon on the Mount: "When you pray, do not be like the hypocrites who love to stand and pray in the synagogues and corners of the streets so that everyone may see them. The reward of such people is the satisfying of their vanity. But you should pray in secret to God from the depth of your hearts. God sees into your souls and He will see you and hear your prayer."

Meekness, justice, sincerity, humility. . . . It was not easy to put these teachings of the Master into practice, and it is no easier in our days than it was then. But we all know that it is only by adopting such principles that men can save themselves from pride, violence, injustice and hatred, from all the evil forces that are tearing them apart and causing so much suffering.

Jesus must by now have been speaking for over two hours. The time has now come to cease and to allow the good people who have listened so attentively to Him to make their way home and to carry His words with them. But there is just one more lesson to be given, so that His teaching will be repeated by those who have had the wonderful privilege of hearing them. Every one of those present must pass on the Word to those about him, so that the Good News may be spread in the land. So, as they make their way down the hill to the lakeshore and disperse to their villages, or set out on their journey to their distant homes, the people, wonderstruck at all they have heard, repeat to each other the simple little sentences in which Jesus had called on them to take part in His work:

"You are the light of the world. Men do not light a candle and put it under a bushel, but upon a candlestick, that it may shine for all that are in the house. So let your light shine before men, that they may see your good works, and glorify your Father, who is in Heaven. . . ."

IX

Why Jesus Worked Miracles

IF THE CROWDS who listened to Jesus found themselves carried
away by the truth and the beauty of His teaching, they were
completely overwhelmed by certain of His acts—His "miracles."
We have already used the word several times; for example, when
we told of how He changed water into wine at Cana or when He
stilled the tempest, but it is a difficult word which needs some ex-
plantation. Many people, including many grownups, do not quite
know what a miracle is. So let us try to make the matter clear.

If you look around you, you cannot but marvel at the wonders
of nature. The regular rising and setting of the sun and moon; the
ordered, twinkling dance of the stars across the heavens; a tiny seed
cast in the earth which in a few weeks germinates and puts forth a
sprout; the branches, leaves and flowers of a tree; a baby, so tiny at
birth, who grows up to be a man—all these are natural wonders
which, if we were not so used to them, would provoke our deep
admiration. All this perfect order of nature and of life has been
planned and arranged by God. In His power He has laid down
His commands and the universe obeys Him. The sun and moon
rise and set, the seed germinates and men grow, always in the same
manner, according to the laws which He has made.

It can be said, therefore, that everything that exists in this world
does so by the grace and wisdom of God. But there are times when
the Almighty Master, instead of allowing things to have their way
according to the ordinary law, intervenes directly in nature. Just
as a watchmaker, by adjusting a wheel, can cause a watch he has
made to go fast or slow, so does God, by intervening in the order
which He has created, bring about happenings which surprise and

confuse men. For example, God has decided that in the natural order it takes six months for a grain of wheat to become an ear; suppose He decided to do this in six minutes, it would be just as easy for Him, but people would be very much surprised. We describe as "miracles" those cases when God Himself visibly intervenes in the ordinary course of nature, so that something quite extraordinary takes place. If we stop to think for a moment, of course, it is no harder for us to accept a miracle—that is, the direct interference by God with the ordinary course of nature—than to accept the innumerable wonders of nature which we see all around us and to which we are so accustomed that we scarcely pay any attention to them.

Jesus, being God, had therefore the power to perform miracles. The laws of nature were as much under His control as the watch is under that of the watchmaker. The question we must ask, and it is a very important one, is *why* should He have performed miracles? *Why* should God interfere with the natural order which He had Himself created? It was most certainly not for the purpose of doing unusual things. It would be ridiculous to imagine Almighty God performing tricks to astonish people, like a magician at a fair. No, when God decides to work a miracle, it is for a very precise and lofty reason. For instance, in the early days of Israel, why did He open the waters of the Red Sea to the Hebrews in their flight from the Egyptians? In this case the miracle was performed in order to save His chosen people destined by Him to teach the true religion to mankind. In the same way we will not find in all His life on earth one instance where Jesus performed a miracle in order to astonish the people. On the contrary, when people demanded one out of mere curiosity, He refused them. When He *did* perform a miracle, it was invariably to give men a lesson in virtue and faith and to make them realize His divine power. Every one of His miracles had a purpose, and it is this purpose which we must try to understand.

You remember, of course, the miracle of the calming of the tempest. Jesus spoke but a few words and the mighty waves, which were threatening to capsize His disciples' boat, subsided instantly. If you had been present you would have been as thunderstruck as the disciples. No doubt you would have asked yourself, as they did, "Who is this man that both wind and sea obey Him?"

Here is the story of another miracle which, if you had been present, would have filled you with admiration and perhaps frightened you a little. One day when Jesus was preaching in the synagogue, a man among those present suddenly burst out with the most horrible cries. He was one of those unhappy creatures whose soul had become possessed by a demon. And as all demons hate God, the poor possessed man raved against Jesus. But as he rolled on the ground in the most horrible convulsions the Master approached him. "Depart from this man!" said Jesus. Instantly it was all over, and the poor afflicted man fell silent and calm, completely cured. Those who were present were stunned with amazement and said wonderingly to one another, "He commands even the demons, and they obey Him!"

There was another type of miracle even more extraordinary. On several occasions Jesus actually raised people from the dead. One day, for instance, a man named Jairus, whose little twelve-year-old daughter was dying, threw himself at Jesus' feet and begged Him to come and cure her. Jesus went with him, but on the way they met a messenger who told them that the child was dead. The poor man burst into tears, believing that now all hope was gone. "Fear not," Jesus said to him. "Believe only, and your child shall live." And, indeed, that is what happened. When they arrived at Jairus' house they found the whole family in mourning. "Weep not," said Jesus, "the maid is not dead but sleeping." The people around only laughed at Him and shrugged their shoulders, for they knew very well that the poor girl was dead. Our Lord, however, came to the couch on which the dead child lay, took her by the hand and said quietly, "Maid, arise!" At once she came back to life, whereupon Jesus told her parents to give her something to eat. Not merely the force of nature and the demons but even death itself obeyed Christ.

This is precisely the first lesson that Jesus taught by His miracles. By them He proved His power, not merely to those who were present at the time, but to all those who would learn of them in the centuries to come. As He Himself said, "The works that I do give testimony that the Father has sent Me." The purpose of the miracles was to persuade men to heed His words and to follow His teaching.

This, however, was not their sole purpose, for in working miracles Jesus did not wish merely to prove that He was God Himself, the Son of the Most High. Consider His words to Jairus, *"Believe only, and your child shall live."* These simple words are of great importance, for they mean, "If you wish Me to grant your prayer, believe in Me." Whatever you ask with your whole heart and soul will, you may be sure, be granted to you, but without faith nothing can be obtained from God.

Take the case of the leper who came to Jesus. He was, poor man, a frightful figure, from whose ravaged face two eyes gazed out in agony. "Lord, if you will, you can make me clean," he cried. Here indeed was utter confidence and belief in Jesus and we can be sure that the leper's appeal was not to be in vain. Jesus stretched forth his hand saying, "I so will! Be made clean." And at that very moment the fearful sickness disappeared.

Then let us see the poor woman who edged her way through the crowds that surrounded the Master. She had been ill for twelve years, suffering from a continued loss of blood that no doctor had been able to cure, although all her money had been spent on medicines and doctors' bills. So great was her faith in Jesus, she did not even try to speak to Him, saying to herself, "If I shall touch only His garment, I shall be healed." Jesus felt her touch and turned around, asking, "Who has touched Me?" Trembling, the poor woman threw herself at His feet. And Jesus said, "Be of good heart, daughter, your faith has cured you." And cured she was, from that very moment.

And we may tell of yet another beautiful and touching scene. One day Jesus and His disciples were in a house, and all around it was a dense crowd of His followers. A poor paralyzed man who

lived in the neighborhood had heard of Jesus and implored his friends to carry him on a stretcher to the Master's feet, so that he could beg to be cured. His friends agreed, but when they got near the house they found it crammed to the doors, so that it was quite impossible to come close to Jesus. The sick man, however, was not going to give up so easily. If it was impossible to enter the house by the door, well, there were other ways. A terrace gave access to the tiled roof, as to this day it does in many houses in the East, so up went the paralytic and his bearers. They tore a hole in the thatch, and through this they lowered the stretcher on ropes, so that at last the sick man lay at the very feet of Jesus. Here indeed was confidence and belief of the kind that the Master could not ignore. He uttered a word, and the helpless paralytic arose from the stretcher, a cured man with full vigor in all his limbs. Once again God had performed a great miracle to reward great faith.

The Gospels contain countless other instances of miracles as loving and compassionate as those we have mentioned. There were many other cripples restored to strength, lepers made clean, blind people made to see again and deaf people to hear. In the two years of His public life, Jesus wrought miracle after miracle to ease the sorrows of mankind. And for all these blessings He asked only one thing: complete and utter faith.

By now, I am sure, you all know what a miracle means and how important it is for us to know and believe in those performed by Christ. But I would now like to explain that these extraordinary deeds had another meaning and that Jesus had another intention in working them. Many of these miracles foretold Christ's plans for the future, and these He wished to reveal only little by little to men. When, for example, He saved His companions from shipwreck on Lake Tiberias He did for them exactly what He does each day for every one of us; He protects and watches over us when life's trials seem too heavy and when even our souls are in danger. When He cured cripples and lepers, He did for them just what He does for us when our souls are sick with grave sins: when we pray to Him with true contrition, we feel ourselves forgiven, cured and cleansed.

Before I finish this chapter I want to tell you of one of Jesus' most beautiful miracles, which reveals matters of great importance. This miracle took place on the shores of Lake Tiberias in the spring of A.D. 29. Jesus had retired to the almost-deserted eastern bank of the lake in order to be alone for a while. But His followers heard of His hiding place and followed Him some eight miles in their anxiety to hear more from Him. He was soon surrounded by the crowd, and once again He preached and cured the sick. Hours went by; the day was drawing to a close. His disciples pointed out to the Master that the people were hungry but that there was no food to be had for them in this desolate place.

"Is there anyone here who has food?" Jesus asked. He was told, yes, but very little, only five barley loaves—and what use would they be for five thousand people? Jesus told the disciples to ask the multitude to sit down. This they did, grouped in hundreds on the slopes of a hill. Jesus took the loaves, blessed them and raised His eyes to heaven in prayer to His Father. Then He gave orders to distribute the bread and also two fishes which He had likewise blessed. Here was a miracle indeed, for every one of the five thousand received his fill. The supply seemed inexhaustible, for, when everyone had eaten to his heart's content, there were twelve baskets of fragments left over! This miracle is called the "Multiplication of the Loaves and Fishes."

Now, what exactly were Jesus' reasons for performing this miracle? First of all, of course, because, in His goodness, He had pity on the hungry multitude. And also because He wished to show favor to those people who had traveled a long distance in such great numbers just to hear Him speak. But He must have had another reason as well. In giving bread to this great crowd, He surely wished to show that He had come to give mankind its true nourishment: food not merely for the body but for the soul. We know that this is true because, a little while later, when certain people spoke wonderingly of the marvel they had witnessed, He said to them, "You come to Me not because of the miracles you have seen, but because you were fed. But I say to you, there is another bread: the bread that comes from God to nourish the souls of men."

Continuing, Jesus said an even stranger thing, "I am the bread of life, and whoever eats of this bread shall live forever. This bread is My flesh which I will give for the life of the world." When He spoke these words, the Apostles did not understand their meaning, for Jesus had not yet fully revealed His intentions to them. But you, my children, when you think of Holy Communion, the spiritual food that is renewed again and again, that tiny wafer of bread which fills you with grace and fervor, you know the inner meaning of Christ's miracle and you know what the Bread of Life is.

X

Jesus Is Opposed: The Death of John the Baptist

"**D**O YOU REALLY BELIEVE in this man, this Jesus of Nazareth? Well, if you do, I don't. Whoever heard of an uneducated workman dabbling in religious matters as though he were one of our learned rabbis who has spent years studying the Scriptures before daring to speak about them? I can tell you our priests and leaders are beginning to keep an eye on Him. He is far too glib with His comments on the sacred Law of Moses. I tell you, this fellow who draws the rabble after Him is an impostor, a false Messias. Indeed, I wouldn't be surprised if He were one of Satan's creatures and if these famous miracles that impress you so much were not worked by witchcraft."

Talk like this began to be whispered throughout Palestine and, unpleasant as it is to have to repeat such words, we must tell of them. Have you ever noticed how in all groups of society, there are to be found one or two malicious, jealous and spiteful people who take pleasure in speaking ill of those others admire? Every time there appears on the scene someone who is finer and more generous of character than the average, you can be sure that these spiteful people will try to run him down and to hinder his efforts to do good. It is sad that this should be, and it shows human nature in a bad light, but it is unfortunately true and it was thus with Jesus.

In contrast to the splendid faith and love He received from so many people, Jesus also had many opponents. It is important to note this because in the end it was these enemies of His who were to organize the abominable plot that led to His death. Jesus, of course, was well aware of their evil intentions, but not for an instant did He allow any thought of danger to turn Him from His mission. Did He not Himself foretell the tragic end that awaited Him? Little did His miserable enemies dream that what they did was to bring Him glory, and that they were able to work against Him only because He, the All Powerful, permitted them to do so.

Jesus' enemies were of all sorts and of various degrees of bitterness. Some were of the suspicious and spiteful type that we all know: people who refuse to believe in the most beautiful of God's works on earth and who did not really believe in all His miracles. Even when they had seen these with their own eyes, or were faced with undeniable proofs, they claimed that the miracles were worked by the Devil and that Jesus was some sort of sorcerer. To them, Jesus replied, "If I am a demon and by Satan work miracles, why do I then cast out demons from the souls of the possessed as you have seen me do? A kingdom divided against itself cannot stand." To this argument His enemies could make no answer.

There were others who just shrugged their shoulders, saying, "He is a troublesome agitator." Even some of His own relations took this view. They called Him a crank and said they dreaded lest He bring discredit on the family. Some even thought that it would be safer to have Him locked up as a madman. It is the fate of all men of genius to be misunderstood by common men, so it was really not very surprising that these unlettered Galilean peasants should have been unable to realize that this cousin of theirs whom they had known since His birth, the son of Joseph the carpenter, was God Himself.

The Gospels tell us of one very significant incident which shows us how jealous and suspicious people tried to do harm to Jesus. Once, when He paid a visit to His native village of Nazareth, the villagers gathered around Him, saying, "Do we not hear that you performed great wonders at Capharnaum and other places? Why not show us Your powers here? Work a miracle for us, the people of Your own country." You can hear the tone of envy, curiosity and even of mockery in their words. Jesus did not do as they asked. He would not perform a miracle just to astonish the country people of Nazareth. So they were furious with Him and gathered around Him uttering threats and insults. Worse still, they hustled Him to a cliff above the village, and it looked as if they intended to throw Him over it. They did not succeed, however, for Jesus escaped by vanishing from their midst. All the same, this was a very revealing incident, and from this Gospel story comes the proverb: "No man is a prophet in his own country."

These particular enemies of Jesus were not very important and they could do Him little serious harm. From another quarter, however, there was a much more formidable opposition. This came from a group of Jews called the Pharisees. You will have to know something about them for it was the Pharisees who were later to prepare the plot against Jesus and to be mainly responsible for His death.

The name "Pharisee" was given to men who boasted that they practiced their religion better than others, and who took pride in showing themselves more pious, self-denying, spiritual and rigid than anyone else, at least so far as appearances went. They constantly went about dressed in mourning. On fast days their faces were pale and drawn, so that everyone could see that they had taken no food. They always took a prominent seat in the Temple so that everyone could observe how fervently they prayed. When they gave alms, you can be sure that they did so in the public streets, so that all the passers-by could witness their generosity.

You can imagine what Jesus thought of all this—Jesus, who always taught His followers to be humble and discreet, to offer their prayers to God from the depths of their hearts instead of seeking the admiration of others. Jesus did not mince his words when talking about the Pharisees. For instance He called them "whited sepulchers," comparing them to tombs that are well kept and shining without but within contain only the dead.

On another occasion He told His followers this story, "Two men went up to the Temple to pray. One of them was a Pharisee, and going right up to the front of the Temple where everyone could see him, he began to pray aloud, 'I thank You, Lord, because you have made me perfect. I fast, I pray, I observe all the religious feasts; indeed I have no faults. I thank You, Lord, for having made me such a true believer.' The second man was a publican, that is, a minor tax and customs official. He stood far back in the Temple where no one could see him, and silently poured out his soul in prayer: 'O God, be merciful to me, a sinner.' " Jesus ended this story by asking, "Which of these two men's prayers was answered by God? Most certainly not that of the Pharisee."

As you can well imagine, remarks like this were by no means pleasing to the Pharisees, and they looked around for ways of taking revenge on Jesus. They began by accusing Him of breaking the sacred Law of Moses which, for a Jew, was a serious crime. The Pharisees paid exaggerated attention to the fine points of the Law. They did not concern themselves much with its great precepts of generosity, charity and love of one's neighbor, insisting rather on a strict observance of its minor rules. For example, they gave all sorts of absurd meanings to the law of Sabbath rest which had been laid down by Moses. They wanted people not only to keep from working on that day, but to do nothing—absolutely nothing. And they said, "It is not lawful to carry a package for more than two hundred yards on the Sabbath. It is not lawful to write to a friend, not even one line. It is not lawful to eat an egg that has been laid on the Sabbath." The very height of absurdity was reached by one Pharisee who solemnly held, "It is unlawful to kill a flea on the Sabbath Day."

Jesus, it is true, paid no attention to these stupid regulations, which had nothing to do with real religion. So the Pharisees started a whispering campaign against Him throughout the country, saying, "You know this Jesus of Nazareth—it is pure sacrilege to say, as some people do, that He is a prophet and even the Messias Himself. Why, the man is a lawbreaker who does not even observe the Sabbath! He performs miracles on that day and quite recently dared to cure a cripple on the day dedicated to the Lord. And His followers are just as bad. They have been seen in broad daylight on the Sabbath breaking off stalks of wheat in the fields and eating them. All this is a grave sin."

Up to now all this criticism and disagreeable talk did not matter much. But, as Jesus' teachings spread and the number of His followers increased, so did the hostility to Him grow greater, and it was to end in tragedy.

The Pharisees were not the only people to be disturbed by Jesus' words and the success of His mission: the rulers of the people now began to show concern. You remember how we explained (in Chapter V) that Palestine in Jesus' time was divided into several portions: the southern province, Judea, was administered by a Roman official, while the north remained under the rule of Herod's son. The Romans naturally were always on their guard against any popular agitation in the territory they occupied, and their guards kept a fairly close eye on Jesus and His followers. In the first part of His public life, however, up to September of the year 29 (see chronological table at the end of this book), Jesus only came to Judea from time to time to attend the great religious festivals, spending the rest of His time in Galilee. It was therefore the ruler of Galilee who was mainly concerned with the new movement in his territory and with the large crowds that assembled there.

The puppet king who ruled Galilee at that time was Herod Antipas, son of the great Herod, and although he was not so cruel as his father, the life he led was almost as bad. His soldiers kept a watch on Jesus and reported back to him all they heard. Herod Antipas was puzzled. What did this Jesus want? He did not seem to covet the throne, and so He could not be very dangerous. The king was not anxious to have Jesus arrested, and so he allowed Him to carry on His mission although at the same time he kept a close watch on Him. It was at this time that Herod Antipas found himself involved in a most distressing affair, the memory of which was long to haunt his dreams.

You remember John the Baptist, of course? After he had baptized Jesus he had continued to preach to the crowds at various places in the Jordan valley. Then suddenly he was arrested by the soldiers of Herod Antipas and thrown into the fortress of Machaerus, above the Dead Sea (see map). There he was held a prisoner for months and months. Why?

Herod Antipas had married his own sister-in-law, after having compelled her to divorce his brother, which was of course very wrong of him. Now, as you know, it was one of the virtues of the Prophets that they openly denounced the sins of the great, even of kings, without fear or hesitation. When, for example, King David,[1] in spite of all his goodness, had committed the horrible sin of having one of his officers killed so that he could marry the man's wife,

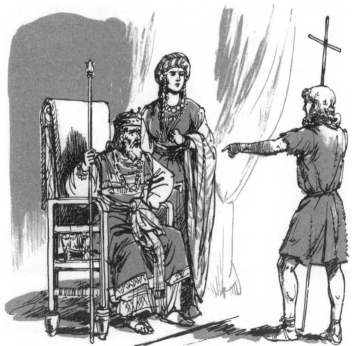

[1] See *The Book of Books,* chapter xi.

the prophet Nathan rose up before him and openly denounced his crime. In like manner, John the Baptist had not hesitated to say to King Herod Antipas, "It is not lawful for you to have your brother's wife!" The wife, Herodias, was furious, and persuaded her weak-willed husband to order John's arrest.

Now one day, when the royal couple were at Machaerus, there was a great banquet and probably the guests drank more than was good for them. Herodias called on her daughter Salome, who was skilled in the dances that are so popular in the East, to entertain the company. So well did Salome dance that the king was enchanted with her. "Ask of me what you will!" he cried, "and I will give it to you." He even made a vow to seal his promise. In reply Salome, prompted by her mother, made this horrible request, doubly horrible when uttered by a young girl: "Give me here in a dish the head of John the Baptist." Herod was extremely displeased at this demand, for he feared the prophet, and in his heart he asked himself if the man of God was not right in what he had said. However, he had given his promise and, not wishing to violate his stupid vow, he gave his orders. An executioner went to John the Baptist's cell and struck off his head. Before the horrified eyes of the guests who, however, were afraid to protest, the bloody head of John was brought in on a big dish.

When word of the tragedy of Machaerus was brought to Jesus, He paused to pray for the man who was His friend and cousin, and who had now been put to death for his courage in defending the law of God in the face of a petty tyrant. Jesus cried out, "I say to you that among all men there was never a greater prophet than John the Baptist."

As for Himself, Jesus knew perfectly well what it might cost a man to speak only the pure Word of God. Knowing that soon His enemies would come together to plot His destruction, He nevertheless continued His work, for it was beyond the power of the Pharisees or of the puppet Herod to prevent Him from saying what He had to say and doing what He had to do.

XI

The Parables of Jesus

WE HAVE LISTENED to Jesus as He delivered His great Sermon on the Mount, so full of wisdom and guidance. We have also heard Him speaking many times in more familiar terms to His disciples and others who thronged around Him. He never missed an occasion to advise His followers how they should act in order to please God and win salvation for themselves. Jesus, however, made use of another unusual and rather picturesque method to explain His teachings, and now I want to tell you about this.

He sometimes spoke in what are called "parables." A parable is a lively little story told against a background that will be familiar to all who hear it. Sometimes the parable is dramatic, sometimes exciting; not unlike the fables of Aesop or of La Fontaine which many of you have read. The Eastern peoples have always been fond of this method of impressing some moral lesson on the minds of their listeners. You yourselves know, when you read say of "The Fox and the Crow" or "The Lion and the Mouse," how easy it is to remember the "moral" of the fable because your imagination has been captured by the animals and people who play their parts in it.

When you read one of the parables from the Gospel, there are two parts of each that you must bear in mind. First of all, there is the story itself with its action, characters and dramatic quality; and then there is the lesson that Jesus meant to convey in telling it. Very obviously Christ was not going to tell stories just to amuse and entertain His listeners. But each of His parables was so well thought out and so perfectly told that both the story itself and the lesson it taught remained fixed in the memory of those who heard it. To this day almost everyone knows the parables of the "Prodigal Son," the

"Good Samaritan," and many others as well. Every important part of Christ's teaching is found in these simple stories which are told in the most lively way imaginable.

"The sower went out to sow his seed. And as he sowed, some fell by the wayside, and it was trodden down, and the fowls of the air devoured it. And others fell upon a rock: and as soon as they were sprung up, they withered away, because they had no moisture. And some fell among thorns and the thorns growing up with it, choked it. But others fell upon good ground, and being sprung up, yielded fruit a hundredfold."

Is not this parable perfect? No one who has ever seen a sower at work and who knows how plants grow can fail to understand these words or the accuracy of the picture they paint. The moral too is very simple, *all* the more so because Jesus Himself has explained it for us—a thing He only rarely did. When His disciples asked Him what the parable meant, He told them:

"The seed is the Word of God. And they by the wayside are they that hear; then the devil cometh, and taketh the word out of their heart, lest believing they should be saved. Now they upon the rock, are they who when they hear, receive the word with joy: and these have no roots; for they believe for a while, and in time of temptation, they fall away. And that which fell among thorns, are they who have heard, and going their way, are choked with the cares and riches and pleasures of this life, and yield no fruit. But that on the good ground, are they who with a good and perfect heart, hearing the word, keep it, and bring forth fruit in patience."

You see how easy it is not merely to understand a parable, but to prove its truth from your own experience. How often we make a thousand good resolutions to work harder, to be more considerate, to behave better to our parents, to be more attentive to our religious duties, only to realize all too soon that we have not kept them. Were these resolutions seeds that were eaten by a bird? Or were they smothered by thorns? Or did they perish on stony ground?

On many other occasions and in different terms, Jesus returned to this most important lesson: that it is not enough to hear the Word of God but that we must put its precepts into practice. And the last is much more difficult. It means that we must always be on our guard, to keep Satan from undoing the task we have begun. To illustrate this lesson, Jesus told another parable, about a man who had sown his field with the very best of wheat. When harvest time came he was surprised and horrified to see that his wheat was all mixed up with cockle, a bitter and evil-smelling weed. What had happened? While the good farmer was asleep, an enemy had stolen into the field and had sowed it liberally with cockle seed. Exactly the same may happen to us if we are not always on our guard.

Do you remember the greatest of all the precepts taught by Jesus, the one He repeated over and over again to the people of His time—and which people in these days would do so well to follow? "Love one another." Jesus taught this lesson many times and in many forms, but the best known is the parable of the "Good Samaritan," one of the most beautiful in the whole of the Gospels.

"A certain man went down from Jerusalem to Jericho. [It was a little-frequented road across a forbidding desert.] He was attacked by thieves who robbed him and left him half-dead on the road. People passed by, among them a priest who saw the poor man lying on the road but paid no attention to him. Then came a Levite, that is, a man employed in the service of the Temple of Jerusalem. He approached the poor victim, listened for a moment and then he too passed on. But finally there came a Samaritan, and he was moved by pity. He bent over the wounded man, pouring oil and wine into his wounds and then bandaging them up. Then, he lifted the man on to his own beast, and led him to the nearest inn. There he saw to it that the man received the best of care. In the morning, before going on his way, the Good Samaritan left with the host a sum of money sufficient to pay for the wounded man's keep, saying, 'Take care of him, and if this money is not enough, I will pay the rest on my return.' " Jesus concluded His parable with the words, "That is how we should show our love for our neighbor."

This is indeed a striking little story, and it is easy to see how deeply it must have impressed those who heard it. The Samaritans were not even true Jews, much less believers. To a Jew, every Samaritan was an enemy, a man to be distrusted. (Earlier in this book we explained this when we were telling about how Jesus met the Samaritan woman at the well and asked her for a drink of water.) What Christ wished to emphasize was that we must not refuse help and generosity even to an enemy or pass by with indifference the misery and suffering of others.

Again and again, this great precept of charity and love is brought home to us through the parables; indeed one finds it everywhere in the Gospels. Above all things Jesus detested, as God detests, selfishness and hard-heartedness. If any man fails to show brotherly love to his neighbor in this life, he can be very sure that he will have to answer to God for it when his time comes. Two parables, both severe in tone, draw our special attention to the view the Eternal Judge will take when the time comes for each of us to appear before Him and when all our deeds on earth will be judged according to the love we have shown our neighbor.

One of these parables tells of the rich and selfish man and of the poor beggar who begged at his gates. This, alas, can happen at all times and in all countries; you can prove it yourself merely by looking around you.

"There once was a rich man who dressed in fine clothing and every day sat down to sumptuous meals. And there was also an unhappy wretch, named Lazarus, who dragged his way through the street near the house, hoping to find something to eat from the crumbs that fell from the rich man's table. Lazarus was so poor and ill that his body was covered with ulcers.

"The two men died and the situation was completely changed. Lazarus, who had suffered so much on earth, was carried by angels up to heaven where God called him to His side, next to the patriarch Abraham. But the selfish rich man was cast into hell, and from the depths of the abyss he cried out to Lazarus, 'Lazarus, I burn! Only dip your finger in water and give me a drop to drink, for I am in torment.'"

A lesson that Jesus often emphasized was that many of those who are first on earth shall be last in heaven, but, on the other hand, those who are poor and suffer on earth shall be welcomed by God. In view of this, one can only marvel that men should continue to be so hard toward one another when they have been plainly told the fate that awaits such conduct in the next world and when they know the words that Jesus will speak to them.

The other parable was really a commentary on a phrase from the "Our Father" which we all repeat every day. "Forgive us our trespasses as we forgive those who trespass against us." The story told is that of a bad servant who was heavily in debt to his master. He went to the latter to beg him to forgive the debt. In his generosity, the master did as he asked. But scarcely was the interview over than the servant met a fellow servant who owed him some trifling sum. Then, forgetful of the kindness he had just received, the ungrateful wretch turned on his fellow servant, seized him by the throat and cried out, "Pay me what you owe me!" And what did the master do? When he heard what was happening, he at once ordered his guards to arrest this wicked man and cast him into the deepest of dungeons. How could he who had been forgiven a heavy debt not forgive the small sum owed to him? This parable teaches that if we want God to forgive us, we must forgive our neighbors.

If some of Jesus' parables were told as a warning of the anger of God against those who treat their neighbors harshly or unjustly, there are many other consoling ones told to give us some understanding of God's love and mercy.

The most famous of those dealing with the goodness of God is that of the Prodigal Son. Here it is:

"There was a man who had two sons. One day the younger of them said to his father, 'Give me now my share of my heritage.' His father agreed, dividing up his goods and giving the son his share. Not many days after, the younger son gathered all he had and went away to a far-off country, and there he wasted all he had in riotous living.

"After he had spent all he had nothing on which to live. Just at this time a famine struck the country. To keep himself from starving, the young man went into the service of a farmer who sent him to guard his flock of pigs. Even there the youth found it so difficult to find food that he often ate the husks that were left by the pigs.

"Finally he began to think of his past follies and he said to him-

self, 'At home, in my father's house, the least of his servants has enough to eat, while here I perish with hunger. I will arise and will go to my father. I will say to him, 'Father, I have sinned against you, and I am no longer worthy to be called your son. Only take me back as the least of your servants.'

"So back the young man went, ragged and miserable. As he drew near to his old home, his father saw him and was overcome by pity. Running toward his unworthy son, he took him in his arms and embraced him tenderly. And calling to his servants he said, 'Bring out quickly a fine robe for my son. Kill the fatted calf so that we may celebrate with a feast. For my son whom I thought dead to me is come to life again. He who was lost has been found.'"

As you well know, this is the treatment we receive from God if, no matter how grave our sins have been, we humbly and sincerely beg His forgiveness. His tenderness and mercy are without bounds for those who admit their sins and implore His pardon. It may even seem surprising to us that God should be so quick to forgive over and over again. During His life on earth various people, including the Pharisees, reproached Jesus with having too much pity for sinners. What was the use, they asked, of leading a virtuous and prudent life unlike the Prodigal Son, if the worst sinner could find pardon? Jesus answered this argument with another parable.

"Which of those among you, if he has a flock of a hundred sheep and loses one, will not leave the ninety-nine and go after the one that is lost? Or who, when he has found it, will not carry it back joyfully upon his shoulders and when he goes home will not call together his friends to rejoice with him? So I say to you, there is more joy in heaven over one sinner that repents than over ninety-nine just men who have no need for repentance."

When we think of Jesus, what lovelier images can we bring to our minds than that of the Good Shepherd who carries us, the lost sheep, back to the house of God? Or else that of the Father, who, from the threshold of His house, opens wide His arms to greet the Prodigal Son?

XII

The Jesus Men Loved

WE HAVE NOW BEEN FOLLOWING for some time in the footsteps of Jesus as He trod the roads of Palestine, and have been reading the wonderful teachings that have been handed down to us in the Gospels. And yet, and you have no doubt noticed this, I have not once made any attempt to describe Him to you or to tell you what He looked like. Indeed, this apparent omission of mine might have confused you were it not for the pictures in this book which will help you to form your own impression of Him.

If I have been silent on this point it is for the very simple reason that my purpose is to tell you about the Gospels, and not once do any of the Gospels make any reference to the Master's physical appearance. It may seem strange, but it is true. Neither Matthew, Mark, Luke nor John give us any hint as to whether Jesus was tall or short, dark or fair, clean-shaven or bearded. They do not describe His voice; in short, they tell us nothing whatever about His appearance. If we reflect, however, we can easily understand this omission. The purpose of the Evangelists when they wrote their Gospels was simply to spread the Good News, that is the divine doctrine taught by the Messias. Did it matter at all whether the Man who taught this doctrine was tall or short, dark or fair? The one thing that mattered to them was the truth of the message taught by Jesus, and they devoted their whole effort to expressing this truth.

This does not mean that we are not entitled to form our own picture of Jesus, just as so many artists have done for nineteen centuries. It seems probable that the splendor of God must have shone through His human form, and that His gaze could pierce to the innermost souls of men. When we read in the Gospel of Jesus' cease-less activities, traveling the length and breadth of Palestine, preach-ing to huge crowds, teaching and directing His infant Church, we are left with the strong impression of a very energetic person, in the full vigor and splendor of healthy young manhood. All the same, when an artist draws a picture of Christ his picture is not so much the real Christ of flesh and blood, of whom we know so little, but rather his own conception of that wondrous figure that each of us carries in his heart.

The Gospels give us a much clearer picture of Christ's daily life and surroundings. We can reconstruct this for ourselves all the more easily because the way of life in Palestine has not changed much in the last two thousand years. When we look at the Galilean peasants of our own day, with their white woolen coats, belted linen tunics, sandaled feet and heads enveloped in the wrapped headdress fall-ing on the shoulders that is now called a *couffieh,* we get a very good idea of the sort of garments worn by Jesus during His life on earth. His diet was that of the humble people of his time: bread, vege-tables, fruit and olives; fish was a luxury and meat was eaten only on feast days. For most of the time people drank plain water; only the better-off were able to afford wine, but they also brewed a sort of beer made with fruit and grain which they called *sicera.* All in all, it was, as you see, a simple and humble mode of living.

The Gospel tells us clearly that Jesus gave up the pleasures of home. He traveled ceaselessly, relying for food and shelter on one friend or another, for such hospitality is never refused in the East. Sometimes He slept in a room of the house or on a terrace; if it was summertime the Son of God laid Himself to rest on a straw pallet or in a hammock, or just simply on a pile of sheepskins or a carpet. Many times He and His disciples slept with their mantles rolled be-neath their heads, under the open sky protected only by His Father and the light of the stars. What a lesson in humility there is for us in this!

Now we come to another important detail—the tongue in which Jesus spoke. When you read His actual words as they are quoted in the Gospels, you must naturally wonder about the language used by Him. This is a question that quite a number of grownups would find it difficult to answer if you asked them. The language Jesus used was Aramaic, a Semitic dialect that was first spoken in northern Syria but later was spread by travelers and merchants throughout Palestine. It was not Hebrew, the ancient tongue of Israel, the sacred language of the Bible, but it resembled it fairly closely. Broadly speaking, Aramaic and Hebrew were used in Palestine at the time of Jesus, much as we use English and Latin today. Normally we talk and write in English, but we use Latin for many prayers and church ceremonies. Jesus therefore spoke in Aramaic, but of course, like every pious Jew who studied the sacred Scriptures, He also knew Hebrew. Apart from that, being God, He could speak in any language He wished.

If the Gospel gives us no clue as to the physical appearance of Jesus, it gives us very precise ideas about His character. And what a wonderfully beautiful character it was, the perfect model for all mankind.

In it there was no trace of falsehood or deceit. What Jesus thought He spoke, simply, clearly, without calculation or subtlety. If He thought "yes" Jesus said "yes"; if He thought "no" He said "no." How very different are we all with the little ruses and white lies that make up so much of our lives and speech. The very first lesson we learn from the study of Jesus' character is the necessity of always seeking and following the way of truth.

To do this takes the utmost courage, a quality that Jesus displayed at all times. Never for an instant did He hesitate to bear witness to the Word of God. It was perhaps imprudent for Him to speak to crowds as He did and to criticize powerful people, but Jesus was not concerned with prudence. His personal safety, even His life, did not matter, only the Word of God which He had come to preach.

Nothing could restrain Jesus from speaking and acting as He thought fit where God's interests were concerned. Sometimes He was almost violent when He saw the Law of God being broken or its principles disregarded. Remember how He called the powerful Pharisees "whited sepulchers" without caring what they thought or whether one day they would plot vengeance against Him?

On another occasion, when He entered the courtyard of the Temple of Jerusalem, Jesus found it swarming with merchants and dealers. There were always too many in this holy place. The money-changers were rattling the coins that they sold to pilgrims who wished to make an offering in the Temple, for such offerings could be made only in coins specially minted by the priests. Dealers clamored for the attention of visitors in order to sell them animals for sacrifice. Altogether it was not a very edifying scene. Jesus was outraged, and what did He do? In righteous indignation He seized a bundle of cords, tied them into a whip and drove out the hucksters, saying to them, "My Father's house is the house of prayer, but you have made it a den of thieves."

Such acts of holy anger were rare. In recording them the Evangelists undoubtedly wished to teach us that cases do occur when, if God's interests are threatened, it is sheer cowardice for us to remain silent and do nothing in face of the threat. Much more frequently, however, the Gospels dwell on the goodness of Jesus, on His infinite understanding and generosity. Indeed the four little books of the Gospel contain so many examples of this nature that it would be impossible for us to mention them all. Every time Jesus came in contact with a suffering human being who implored His help, He had pity and came to his aid. There is no human misery that cannot find consolation in the heart of Jesus. Truly the essential part of the Good Tidings which Jesus brought to men was His message of love.

One day, one of his followers approached Jesus and asked Him, "Master, which is the greatest commandment in the law?" Jesus replied unhesitatingly, "You know it well; it is the first commandment of all, given to Moses by God Himself: 'Thou shalt love the Lord thy God with thy whole heart and with thy whole soul and

with thy whole mind.' This is the greatest and the first commandment. And the second is this: 'Thou shalt love thy neighbor as thy-
self.'" Make no mistake about it, these two commandments are
really one, for love of God and love of one's neighbor is the same
thing.

There were many who benefited during Christ's lifetime from
His boundless love for men. We find in the Gospels many instances
of those who loved Jesus and who were loved by Him. When we
think of it, is it not astonishing that Jesus Christ, the Son of God
who was God Himself, should have shown affection and friendship
for mere mortal men like ourselves? That He should have taken
pity on the sick and the crippled and have had ready words to con-
sole and comfort those in sorrow? What a comfort it is for us to
know that this was so; the thought of it is sufficient to lift up our
hearts in our darkest moments.

You have only to open the Gospel almost at random to find
such instances. There is the story of John, the youngest of the
Apostles. For him Jesus had such affection that once, after a meal
that came at the end of a long journey, He allowed the tired youth
to lay his head on His shoulder and sleep. Then we have the family
in Bethany, the sisters Martha and Mary and their brother Lazarus, who were such good friends of the Master that He dropped in
to visit them at all times and frequently stayed in their house as
their guest. What happiness there was in that house when Jesus
appeared! Martha bustled about her household tasks, while Mary
remained with Jesus to keep Him company and to hear Him
speak. . . .

Then there was the day when—after He had been preaching
and working cures for sick people—the children surrounded Jesus.
They too had heard of the Master and loved Him dearly. Fearing
that they would tire Him, one of His disciples said to them, "Go
away now and do not weary the Master with your chatter!" Jesus,
however, heard him and came to the rescue of His young friends.
"Suffer the little children to come unto Me," He said. The little

children came near and He caressed them tenderly. Then he took the occasion to teach a lesson to the elders, "Unless you become as little children, that is, as pure and innocent as you were in your early childhood, you will not enter the Kingdom of heaven. . . ."

On another occasion Jesus was dining with a wealthy man. As was the custom of the time, the guests were reclining on couches as they ate, and their feet were bare. During the meal a woman named Magdalen, who had not a very good reputation in the neighborhood, entered the room and approached the Master. What was she going to do? Kneeling beside Him, she poured a flask of costly perfume over His feet and, weeping, dried them with her long hair. The host was indignant at the interruption. He was about to order Magdalen out of the room when Jesus stopped him. He knew the love that inspired her actions and, with infinite tenderness, He spoke to her, forgiving her her sins.

And here is the story of little Zacheus, the publican. One day Jesus was passing through Zacheus' home town, Jericho, surrounded as usual by a huge crowd. The publican wanted desperately to see the Master, but did not try to approach Him. Was he not just a tax gatherer, disliked by everyone? He was so small that he could not even see Jesus over the heads of the crowd. Then he had a bright idea. He climbed a tree, and from its branches he could gaze at Jesus to his heart's content. But Jesus had seen him too. He read in Zacheus' heart the deep love that had prompted his action. "Zacheus, make haste and come down," He called out gaily, "and make haste to go home. For today I will sup with you, my good Zacheus, because of the love you have shown for me."

The Gospels are so full of incidents of this kind that we could continue to tell about them for pages and pages. Reading them, each of us can say to himself, "How I too would have loved Jesus, had I lived in His days and had the good fortune to meet Him. Had I been there perhaps His gaze might have fallen upon me, and I could have run to His arms like the children, or have welcomed Him to my house like Zacheus the publican. . . ."

Well, that is still possible, for the passing centuries have not changed Christ's love for man, that is, for each and every one of us. In eternity, where He reigns at the right hand of the Father, He shows to each succeeding generation the same loving tenderness that He displayed toward those who knew Him during His life on earth. Of this we have absolute proof, for did He not say, "This is the greatest love a man can show, that he should lay down his life for his friends?" Even more than by His words and deeds, Jesus proved the immensity of His love for men by the sacrifice of His death. We now approach the story of the supreme proof of His love that the Messias gave by His death for the salvation of us all.

XIII

Jesus in Judea:
The Raising of Lazarus

IT WAS IN THE AUTUMN of the year 29 (see table of dates at end of book) that Jesus left Galilee, the much-loved province of His childhood where He had passed so many happy days. He was to spend the rest of His days on earth in Judea, in southern Palestine. Looking at these two provinces on the map, it may seem to you that there could be little difference between them so close are they to each other. And yet in fact they are completely different.

Galilee, you will remember, is a land of rolling hillsides and fertile plains, where charming scenery surrounds the blue Lake of Genesareth. By comparison with this gentle pastoral scene Judea looks grim indeed. It is barren, rocky and parched by the sun. The hard blue sky looks down on vast stretches of desert where the bare red hills are devoid of all vegetation and look like the waves of some petrified sea. It seldom rains there, and when it does, the showers falling in torrents sweep away all fertile soil, leaving only the bare rock. Once spring has passed, the countryside is a uniform dusty gray.

It is, as you see, a country well fitted to be the scene of tragedy. And, at the time of which we speak, it was destined to be the scene of the greatest tragedy of all time. The people of Judea shared the character of their country, for they were for the most part bitter, gloomy and severe. There were exceptions, of course. There were among them warm-hearted and generous souls whose hearts were filled with faith and hope, and who already knew and loved Jesus. But on the whole, these southern Jews lacked the rough but honest simplicity and the simple faith of the Galilean farmers and fisher-men, and all too often they were conceited and proud.

Why, then, did Jesus ever come to this country? First of all, be-cause He wished to make His message known throughout all Pales-tine. Having preached so much in the north he now naturally wished to do the same in the south.

But even more than this, Jesus came to Judea because Jerusalem was there. I can hardly explain to you all that Jerusalem meant to the believing Jew of that period. To him it was something far more than the capital city of Judea; it was the place where God Himself dwelt in His Temple. It was the city, holy above all others, where for a thousand years Jesus' ancestors had worshiped the Almighty, had sung before His altar, and had suffered persecution in defense of their faith. In the far-off unhappy days of their exile in Mesopo-tamia, the Israelites in their grief had composed a magnificent prayer in memory of their Holy City: "If I forget thee, O Jerusalem, let my right hand be forgotten. Let my tongue cleave to my jaws, if I do not remember thee."

It would be unthinkable therefore that Jesus should not come to Jerusalem to proclaim publicly who He was and the message He had come to preach. He knew very well that in coming to the capi-tal He was running a much greater risk than if He continued to preach in a remote province. But what did danger matter to Him? In His divine knowledge of future events, he knew very well the fate that was to befall Him in Jerusalem, but it was also His will that these things should come to pass.

The few months that Jesus spent in Judea between the autumn of the year 29 and the spring of 30 passed in much the same way as the preceding ones He had spent in Galilee. We see the Master per-forming the same deeds and speaking much the same words. He cured cripples and restored sight to the blind. The touching epi-sode that we have already mentioned of Jesus' encounter with the humble little publican Zacheus took place at Jericho in Judea. It was to Judean audiences that Jesus told many of His most beautiful parables.

As always, Jesus never let slip an opportunity for instructing those around Him. One day, for instance, a howling mob dragged a trembling and unhappy woman before Him, all the time yelling insults and abuse at her. They cast her down at His feet. Of what was the woman accused? Of a very grave sin, so serious that the penalty for it laid down by Moses was death by stoning. The mob which had dragged the wretched woman to Him now asked Jesus insolently what they should do, thinking that thus they could lay a trap for Him. If He said "She must die," the words would appear cruel when coming from the mouth of one who always preached forgiveness. If, however, Jesus said, "Forgive her," He would lay Himself open to the charge of disobeying the Law of Moses. What was He to do? Jesus looked first at the woman huddled on the ground and then turning His gaze on her accusers, He said simply, "He that is without sin among you, let him first cast a stone at her." What happened then? The frenzied crowd lowered their eyes, for Jesus' simple phrase had given them something to think about. "Without sin? . . ." What human being is so free of sin that he dare to pass judgment on another? Little by little the mob withdrew, so that the poor woman crouched alone at the Master's feet, hardly daring to believe that she had been spared.

During Jesus' sojourn in Judea there took place two particularly important events which we must now consider. One day Jesus was alone with some of His closest companions on one of those heights from which one can see a great distance and where the immensity of the horizon gives some idea of the immensity of God. Jesus, as He often did, commenced to pray. The Apostles watched Him with awe. His face turned toward heaven and His whole countenance shining with love, He lost Himself in a mysterious conversation with the Father. Waiting until He had finished, one of His disciples said to Him, "Lord, teach us to pray, for we would pray as you do."

You must understand that at this time the forms of prayer used by the Jews were very complicated and difficult. Most of them had been prepared by the Pharisees, so you can well imagine that they were far from simple.

Jesus responded to the Apostles' request, and in order to teach them He recited aloud:

"Our Father who art in heaven, hallowed be Thy name. Thy Kingdom come, Thy will be done on earth as it is in heaven. Give us this day our daily bread. And forgive us our trespasses as we forgive those who trespass against us. And lead us not into temptation, but deliver us from evil."

Is this not a wonderful prayer, marvelous in its beauty and simplicity? Perhaps you are so used to reciting it, you pay little attention to what you are saying. . . . But now try reading it over slowly, as though for the first time, and think carefully about each of its short phrases. If you do, you will realize that it would be impossible to pray better in such a few words. It contains everything that we could possibly wish to express to God: first of all that we adore and love Him; that we hope to see His laws obeyed on earth as they are in heaven. Next we tell of our need from Him for what is necessary for our daily life—food, drink and other things. After that, we find in the prayer the essence of all that Jesus has taught us: that God will pardon our sins to the extent that we will pardon those who sin against us; that to love God we must love our neighbor; in fact that love of God and love of our neighbor is the same thing. Finally, we beg God to deliver us from evil. (And all of us know how vitally we need His aid in this.) That is all, and it is enough.

Truly, when we read over slowly the few lines of the Our Father and marvel at their grandeur and wisdom, we can but feel that these are divine words to which God cannot turn a deaf ear.

The other great event in this period of Christ's life, and one of the most famous in the whole of the Gospel, was the raising of Lazarus. You remember Lazarus, of course? He was the brother of Martha and Mary who always had such a warm welcome in their

house for Jesus.[1] One day the two sisters sent word to Jesus, "Your friend Lazarus is grievously ill. . . ." This message was enough, for Martha and Mary knew Jesus and knew that there was no need to say more. On hearing this Jesus set out at once for the house of his sick friend at Bethany. But while He was on the way Lazarus died, and on His arrival Jesus learned that he had been buried four days previously. Martha, who had hastened to meet Him in order to tell Him the sad news, said to Him sadly, "Lord, if You had been here, my brother would not have died." Knowing well the infinite power of their Friend, she added quickly, "But now also I know that whatsoever You will ask of God, God will give it to You."

You see what Martha was suggesting. She did not dare to demand a miracle but . . . if it was possible . . . if it was Jesus' will. . . . "Your brother shall rise again," replied Christ quietly. Martha was

[1] This Lazarus had no connection with the Lazarus who figured in the parable of the Rich Man which you have read earlier in this book.

overwhelmed by these simple words. It could not be! It was too wonderful to be true, and so words failed her. But Jesus continued, "I am the Resurrection and the Life: he that believes in Me, although he be dead, shall live."

Jesus asked to be led to the tomb. It was blocked by the heavy round boulder, rather like a millstone, that is used to seal tombs in Palestine. Jesus ordered it to be rolled back. When this was done, the entrance to the cave appeared; a small entrance hewn out of the vertical rock that led to the burial chamber itself. Almost overcome with emotion Jesus prayed fervently to God, "Father, I thank You, for I know You have heard Me. And I know that You hear Me always, but because of the people who stand about, I have said it, so that they may believe that You have sent Me." Then in a loud voice, He cried out, "Lazarus, come forth!"

In an instant—and what an amazing instant it was—the dead man came forth. He appeared at the entrance of the tomb, his feet and hands tied in bands, as was the Jewish custom, and his face still covered by his shroud. For a moment his friends stood thunderstruck, then they rushed forward and tore away his bonds. Lazarus' face was pale, but his eyes were open and full of light. It was true, he was a living man!

Jesus had already performed similar miracles in Galilee, and Lazarus was at least the third person He had restored to life. Christ had, however, a very definite purpose in the case of Lazarus. This was, as He said, to prove to people that He was God's envoy and master of death itself. He did this because He knew that very soon His friends' and followers' faith in Him would be put to a most terrible test. When that day came, they would be reassured in recalling the raising of Lazarus, and in repeating the words He had used to Martha, "I am the Resurrection and the Life." They would remember He had conquered death.

As you can well imagine, miraculous events like this did not pass unnoticed. Bethany lies only a few miles from Jerusalem, and word of the miracle must have spread through the streets of the capital almost as soon as it took place. No doubt paid spies watched Jesus and reported carefully to His enemies everything that He did or said. For Jesus had enemies in Judea just as we know He had in Galilee, but in Judea they were more numerous and more bitter against Him. The Pharisees, in particular, had great influence in Jerusalem and all the surrounding district. They held many official positions, particularly in the "Sanhedrin," that is the official body which administered and controlled the affairs of the religious community of Israel. These people made the same charges against Jesus as had been made in Galilee: that He had broken the Law of Moses, that He did not observe the Sabbath, that He was a sorcerer and a demon. . . . It was the same old story. Some of them, however, were more clever and declared, "He claims to be the Son of God, as though any man has the right to call himself God. It is a blasphemy, a horrible blasphemy!" And so the hostile rumors began to spread.

What a sad contrast there is between the gentle goodness of Jesus and the malicious whispering campaign and slanders of His enemies. They laid traps for Him, asking Him questions that might force Him into what could be called real blasphemy or at least an expression of impiety or disloyalty which could justify His arrest. For, after all, they knew that unless they could find some precise reason to arrest Him, they ran the risk of angering public opinion, which admired and respected Jesus.

Jesus, of course, never allowed Himself to fall into the traps laid for Him. He had a perfect reply for all questions put to Him. When, for instance, His questioners showed Him a Roman coin and asked, "Is it lawful for us to pay tribute to the Romans?" He at once saw the snare. If He said, "No," He would be denounced to the Roman authorities as a rebel. If He said "Yes," He would be accused of siding with the invaders who oppressed the Jews. But Jesus gave the perfect answer, "Render to Caesar the things that are Caesar's, and to God the things that are God's."

And so the Pharisees, unable to find an excuse to justify Jesus' arrest, continued to spy on Him, to follow Him and await their chance. . . .

XIV
Triumph and Tragedy

A ND NOW THE SPRINGTIME had come, balmy and sunny, loud with bird song and fragrant with the scent of flowers, as it is to this day in Palestine. Along the wayside and in the crevices of the rocks bloomed the green leaves and mauve blossoms of the wild iris, and everywhere the silk-petaled anemones bloomed in purple splendor. Scented breezes blew across the countryside, and at nightfall the hills were ablaze with the bonfires that traditionally announced the approach of the Paschal festival.

It was the eve of the Passover, the great yearly festival of the Jews, which for countless centuries had commemorated their ancestors' departure from Egypt and the miraculous help given by the Most High to His chosen people in this escape from Pharao.[1] The ceremonies of the Passover had never changed since Moses first instituted them; they consisted of eating lamb roasted on a spit and seasoned with herbs, the meal being accompanied by prayers and hymns in honor of the Lord. To join in the ceremonies, hundreds of thousands of Israelites, not merely from Palestine but from abroad, made their way by caravan or by sea in interminable processions and took the road to Jerusalem, chanting the Psalms of Israel as they went.

Just imagine the bustle and animation of the Holy City at this time of the year! The pilgrims were everywhere. They not merely filled every hostel and inn or stayed with friends and relatives, but camped in the squares and streets of the city, under the city walls or in tents or huts of branches scattered all over the surrounding hills. It was a picturesque and lively scene . . . and a very noisy one.

[1] See *The Book of Books,* chapter VII.

At all events, the Passover celebrations offered an excellent opportunity to anyone who had a message to address and be listened to by a very large audience. It was for this reason that, on the approach of the feast, Jesus went to stay quite close to Jerusalem, either with His friends at Bethany, or on a hill called Mount Olivet which overlooks the city from the east. (See map of Jerusalem at the end of the book.) From either place He had easy access to the city and to the Temple courtyard where He could count on finding huge crowds ready to listen to His teaching.

And so the scene was set for this week, the last of Jesus' human life on earth. It was the week which, because of the events that took place during it and the manner in which they came about, we now call "Holy Week."

"Hosanna, Hosanna! Let us glorify the Lord. Blessed is He who comes in the name of the Lord, the King of Israel. Hosanna! The reign of David is at hand and his son is among us."

We can almost hear the thunderous welcome that echoed along the road leading from Mount Olivet through the Cedron valley to the Temple. The road was packed with people shouting and singing. Some of them cut branches from the trees to strew on the ground; some waved palms in acclamation. Many tore off their cloaks and spread them on the road, thus making an immense carpet. But what is all the excitement about? For whom is this rapturous welcome intended?

We have not far to look, for here He comes, the Man they call the Messias, the son of David, riding an ass like any humble peasant. It is Jesus, and the crowd is overwhelmed by the majesty of His bearing, the light that shines from His countenance and the nobility of the words that fall from His lips. The story of His amazing miracles—above all the raising of Lazarus after he had been four days in his grave—had gone before Him into Jerusalem, carried there by the processions of pilgrims who were coming from all sides. Word of the wonders wrought by Jesus passed from mouth to mouth; and

people told each other that surely here was proof enough that He was truly the Messias. And so they poured out to meet Him on the road from Bethany. . . . This took place on Sunday the 2nd of April in the year 30, and in memory of the tumultuous reception given to Him this Sunday is now called "Palm Sunday."

Needless to say, the Pharisees and other enemies of Jesus were not at all pleased by the demonstrations. Some of them even approached Jesus, bidding Him to silence His followers. Jesus smiled gently and answered them, "If they should hold their peace, the very stones would cry out." And He calmly continued His progress.

He approached the city. Before Him he saw, across the valley of the Cedron, the mighty walls built by Herod, and above them, reaching toward the sky, the proud outline of the Temple with its massive colonnades and towers, gilded and many-colored. Jesus entered the Temple precincts by a gate called "the Golden Gate," followed by the cheering and joyful crowd.

He went to the courtyard reserved for the prayers of the faithful, and there He called upon His Father and spoke to Him. What did Jesus say? Knowing all things, He knew that His present triumph would not last long, that the acclamations of the crowd would soon die down, and they would quickly abandon Him. It was of this that He spoke to His Father, telling Him of the anguish that gripped His heart even at this moment when things seemed to be going so well for Him. At the same time, however, He made no attempt to escape His fate; He accepted in advance the sacrifice which He was called upon to make. He cried out, "Father, glorify Thy Name!" At this moment, the voice of the Almighty spoke from Heaven like a peal of thunder. The listening crowd knew well that this was no ordinary thunder—and besides there were no clouds in the sky. They fell silent in awe and wonder. Who could doubt that this Man to whom God replied was Himself the Son of God, the Envoy of the Most High?

So passed this wondrous day of spring, this day when everything testified to the glory of Jesus. Never perhaps in His whole public life had He been so surrounded by love and joy. All day long under the colonnades of the Temple the crowds listened to His noble and profound teachings. Even after the sun had gone down in the west, behind the three towers of the Temple wall, numerous listeners crowded around Him, untiring in their anxiety to hear what He had to say. Who could ever have dreamed that all this glory would vanish so soon, and that before the week was over the hero of that Sunday would be a pitiable figure of defeat?

As you go through life you will notice (and indeed at school you may have noticed already) that people tend to admire and respect those who appear to be strong, powerful and successful. As the old proverb puts it, "In fair weather you will have many friends, but you will find yourself alone in the storm." The crowds thronged around Jesus on His day of triumph, but how many would remain faithful to Him when danger loomed near?

And yet Jesus had been at pains to make His followers understand that it would not be by earthly splendor, fame or power that His mission on earth would be accomplished. You will remember how often in the preceding years He had foretold His tragic fate, His arrest, His Passion and even His death on the cross. But His followers were unwilling to believe what He said about these matters. This is understandable. They could not bring themselves to accept the fact that Almighty God had chosen to suffer and die. It was too painful for them to picture their friend, their Master, suffering horrible tortures and dying a shameful death like the vilest of criminals. . . . When Jesus spoke of these matters they preferred to think they mistook His meaning or, better still, they chose not to think of the subject at all.

Jesus, however, even in His days of triumph, reminded them ceaselessly of the coming tragedy. He many times tried to make them realize the necessity of the sacrifice He was about to make. Taking, as He often did, a country scene as an example, He said to His disciples, "Unless the grain of wheat dies, it will not bring forth grain. But if it is buried in the earth, it will yield a rich harvest." We know now what Jesus meant by this: that His death, burial and Resurrection would complete His teaching to mankind. But at the time, who could have guessed this?

Again, when the sun was setting behind the Temple towers and the sky was turning red, Jesus raised His hand toward heaven and cried out, "The light will not long be with us!" His disciples looked at each other in bewilderment, for they knew that every word He spoke had a profound meaning, but what that meaning was they could not guess. Perhaps they had forgotten that He had told them that He Himself was the Light. Gently, speaking as a friend among friends, Jesus continued, "Walk while you have the light. Believe in the light, that you may be the children of light." It was all very confusing and disturbing.

So passed the first three days of the week, and so far there was no sign of any of the grave happenings foretold by Christ. Installed in a corner of the Temple, He continued to preach to all who came to hear Him. The smallest happening was used by Him to drive home some deep and important lesson. For instance, He drew attention to a poor widow who humbly approached the Temple offering-box and placed in it a small coin, and He exclaimed, "Truly I say to you, that this poor widow's offering is more pleasing to God than any other, for while others gave from what they had to spare, she has given to the Lord from what she needed."

On Tuesday evening, however, Jesus made a dramatic announcement. On their way back to Mount Olivet, He and His disciples had passed by the foot of the immense Temple walls. One of His followers had commented on the huge blocks of masonry which rose some ninety feet to support the terraces above. Afterward the little band gazed down from the olive-clad slopes of the hill on the splendors of the Holy City, its buildings bathed in the light of the setting sun. Suddenly Jesus stretched out His hand toward the city and cried out in a voice choked with emotion:

"I say to you, there shall not be left of all these things a stone upon a stone. Jerusalem, Jerusalem, what woe will be yours because you kill those whom God has sent to you! Your houses will be left desolate and your people will weep bitter tears."

The disciples looked at each other in amazement. What did Jesus mean? What terrible disaster lay in store for the Holy City? Jesus was looking forty years into the future and foretelling the siege of Jerusalem by the Romans as punishment for a Jewish uprising. He foresaw the burning of the Temple, and the almost entire destruction of the city. "These things," said Jesus, "shall come to pass before the present generation is gone. Heaven and earth shall pass away, but My word shall not pass away."

Did Jesus mean that it was only the people of Jerusalem who would have to account to God for their sins? No, not they alone. All men, everywhere, who spurned Jesus' message and refused to obey His law would in the end be judged by God according to their good deeds and their bad ones. Continuing His prophecy, the Master went on to speak of that wonderful and terrible day when, at the end of the world, the Son of God would return to earth in all His power and majesty, surrounded by His angels, when every human soul would appear before Him for judgment. On that day those who had in life been hard-hearted, cruel and unjust would be condemned by Him and banished into everlasting fire; but those who had led good lives and shown justice and mercy to their fellows would be welcomed by Him to His Father's Kingdom.

As His awestruck disciples pondered His sayings in silence, Jesus gently went on to explain matters to them:

"When Christ returns, He will say to His faithful, 'When I was hungry you gave Me to eat; and when I was thirsty you gave Me to drink. I was a stranger and you took Me in; I was naked and you clothed Me.' And the faithful will cry out: 'But Lord, when did we do all these things? Never had we the joy of giving you food and drink, of sheltering or clothing you.' And Christ will answer: 'In truth, I say to you that each time you did any of these things to the humblest of your fellow men, you did it to Me.'"

How consoling are these words of Jesus. Even while He warns us of the terrible punishment that awaits the wicked, for those responsible for His death, for those who reject and betray His teachings, He speaks to us with love and tenderness. He gives to each of us the key that will open His heart to us: as He so often said, this was love of our neighbor, charity and mercy.

XV

The Plot Against Jesus

WHO WERE THOSE shadowy forms that slipped so furtively through the dark alleys and lanes of Jerusalem? They moved rapidly, their faces hidden by their cloaks as they glided silently up and down the stairways of the hilly streets, hugging the shadows as though afraid the clear light of the moon would reveal their evil purpose. They were all moving in the same direction through the lower quarters of the town and then, through the Potter's Gate and up the hill that faced it. There was situated the isolated country residence of the High Priest, Caiphas. This secluded spot was well suited for a secret meeting and it was here that these night visitors assembled.

Present at this secret meeting were most of the leaders of the Jewish community: the High Priest and his family, the upper clergy of the Temple, Pharisees and doctors of the law, specialists in religious matters, in fact all those who had been made uneasy and angry by Jesus' teachings. For it was Jesus and His actions that were the subject of discussion; it was against Him they were plotting.

"The impertinence of the man, speaking like that in broad daylight, just when Jerusalem is packed with pilgrims for the festival!"

"For days now this wretched impostor has been speaking in the sacred precincts of the Temple itself. And the worst of it is, that there are always crowds about Him; the people are so credulous. . . ."

"They claim that He has cured the sick and restored sight to the blind. What devil's sorcery is this?"

"More than that, some of those crazy followers of His claim that at Bethany He raised a dead man, Lazarus, to life."

"What utter rubbish! As for raising a dead man to life, by the time we're finished with Him, He'll have an opportunity for practicing His powers upon Himself. And as for the resurrected Lazarus, we'll have to send him back to his tomb and make sure that, this time, he stays there."

"It's all very fine to talk like that, but it will not be so very easy to do as you say. He is always surrounded by crowds of admirers who guard Him carefully. The other day, two Temple guards who were sent to throw Him out made no attempt to do so. They came back and said that He spoke so beautifully and said such wonderful things that some strange power seemed to come out from Him."

"All the same, it is time, and high time, too, that we take some active steps against this false Messias. If we allow Him to go on as He is going, who knows how much more trouble He is going to cause us?"

Such, more or less, were the opinions exchanged at this midnight meeting. Its purpose, as you see, was to plot some means of putting an end to Jesus' activities.

You may well ask the reason for the bitter hatred of the Jewish leaders for Jesus. Why should they hate, even to the point of planning to kill Him, this Man who throughout the years of His public life had always shown Himself so loving, so generous and so merciful toward all forms of human suffering?

There were many reasons, some of which we have already seen for ourselves: sordid jealousy; the fear of Jesus becoming too popular a figure, and perhaps even taking over religious functions. Then there was the furious enmity of all those whose faults had been publicly rebuked by Jesus; their hypocrisy, their pride, their love of honors and worldly riches. The High Priests who had enriched themselves and their families from Temple property hated Jesus just as much as did the Pharisees. The latter would never forgive Him for his famous "whited sepulchers" comparison and His other criticisms of them. The people whose virtues Jesus had praised were the meek, the humble and the poor, and these unfortunately had not been invited to the meeting at Caiphas' house.

Of course no mention was made of these base and sordid motives at this evil council. They were nevertheless present in the hidden hearts of everyone there. On the surface, however, much more respectable reasons were given for the proposed attack on Jesus. For example, He was held up as a political threat. "If we do not put a stop to His activities, He will continue to draw crowds and to arouse the rabble. And what will the Romans say about this? If once the Procurator loses patience, the whole city may suffer. If he should loose his soldiers on us God knows what might happen!"

Then, and this was even more serious, the old religious grounds for attacking Jesus were revived. "He claims to be the Son of God! This is worse than blasphemy. Has any man the right to proclaim himself God? Our father Moses definitely forbade such idolatry. And, mark you, Jesus' actions are deliberately intended to make people believe Him to be God. He claims to cure in the name of God. To a paralytic whom He pretended to cure He said, 'Your sins are forgiven you,' as though He, a humble man, almost a beggar, had the power to forgive sins like Almighty God. . . .''

All the same, there is something very hard to understand in all these indignant protests. The Israelites had, after all, been awaiting for centuries and centuries the coming of the Messias; they cherished in their hearts the hope that one day they would see Him with their own eyes. And yet, when He did appear, many of them refused to acknowledge Him and looked upon Him as an agitator and a sacrilegious fraud. But you will remember that in Chapter V of this book we have explained how things happened this way.

The Jews, as you know, differed greatly as to the form in which the Messias would appear. Some believed that He would come as a mighty and terrible king, mightier than Solomon and braver than David, a king who would lead all the men of Israel against their oppressors. Others, however, relying on certain texts of the Bible, formed quite a different picture of the Envoy of the Most High.

They saw Him as a poor man like all other poor men—humble and meek, a victim who would sacrifice Himself to redeem the sins of the world.

Now it must be admitted that the second version was much less popular in Israel than the first. It was only natural and according to human nature that this should be so. It was understandable that the Jewish people, who for five centuries had been under the heel of one foreign conqueror after another, should dream of revenge on their enemies. So, when Jesus appeared as a simple, humble Galilean workman, the son of a carpenter, the leaders of Israel said to each other, "No, this Man cannot possibly be the true Messias. He is not the great king and mighty warrior who will lead our armies to victory over all our enemies. By claiming to be the Messias He is deceiving the people and killing their hopes for liberation in the future. He is a traitor to our cause and should be put to death!"

How little they knew, these poor people so puffed up with human pride, that this same Jesus was not merely the meek and humble Man at whom they sneered but was also the All-Powerful, the Master on whom depended all the kings of the earth, the true and glorious Messias. Still less did they realize that if He allowed Himself to be harmed by them it was because He so willed it.

The discussion had been going on for some time when Caiphas the High Priest rose and called for silence.

"Understand this clearly," he cried, "for this is a matter that concerns the welfare of our people. This Man must die!"

The assembly was stricken silent. It is a grave and terrible thing to decide on a man's death, particularly when, as in this case, it was clear that this Man was guiltless of any crime. But all the members of the evil council were in the grip of the most wicked emotions that can enslave the human soul: hatred, fear, jealousy and pride. So it was decided that Jesus, the self-styled Messias, should die. It was now a matter of settling the details.

Said one, "It will not be easy to arrest Him among all those fanatical followers of His. If we try to seize Him in public, in the Temple for example, we may easily provoke a riot and then we will have the Romans to deal with."

Discussions raged about this point, for everyone realized that Jesus' arrest would be no easy matter. No one even knew where He spent the night, and it was probable that He changed His lodging each evening. Nevertheless, the arrest would have to take place at night when He would be alone. . . .

Then one of those present made signs to Caiphas that he wished to speak. "I know one of Jesus' followers," he said, "one of the twelve who never leave His side. Judas is his name, and he comes from Carioth in the south. He seems dissatisfied with the way things are going. The last time I met him he told me he was tired of always running along the roads after Jesus. He seemed to think it was a silly business and had lost all hope of ever seeing Jesus proclaimed King of Israel."

"That would suggest that Judas has some sense left. Find him! Bring him to us quietly so that his companions know nothing about it. Tell him we will pay well for his help."

This is almost fact, but it is true: among the Twelve, among those who had been Jesus' closest friends from the very beginning, whom He had Himself chosen and in whom He had shown such great trust, there was a traitor. Since the days when the Gospels were first written and throughout the countless generations when men have studied them, no one has ever been able to explain fully the dark and fearful reasons for this wretched man's treachery. What had Judas Iscariot hoped for when he first became one of Jesus' companions? Had he perhaps expected the immediate triumph of the Master and a seat for himself among the ministers of the King of Israel? St. John tells us that Judas was a thief and that he stole from the common purse entrusted to his care. But if he were merely a common thief, would it not have paid him better to go on pilfering rather than to betray his Master? Here indeed is a mystery.

It is equally strange that Jesus, who knew all things, should have allowed Judas to remain with Him to the end. However, on several occasions He made it plain that He knew what was going on. One day He said to the Twelve, "One of you is a devil!"

If Jesus kept Judas among His followers it was because He wished to do so, and this is a mystery that we cannot explain. Judas the criminal, the most frightful traitor ever to walk on earth is, in a way, an example of what each of us can become if he betrays God or, in a lesser degree, abandons himself to evil ways. Jesus has given us His love and taught us the way to salvation, but He has left us free to spurn His love and disobey His teaching if we wish to do so. Every human soul who betrays Jesus is helping to turn Him over to His enemies, just as Judas helped them to put Him to death.

Try to imagine the horrible scene that took place on another night, no doubt on Wednesday of that week. The plotters were again assembled in Caiphas' country house on the Hill of Evil Council. Out of doors, the city was bathed in the gentle radiance of the almost full moon, and the scene was so peaceful that one wonders how man could be so wicked in a world that God has made so beautiful. The door of the house opened and there entered the man who had earlier spoken of Judas. Before him, he pushed another figure. His features distorted and his lips twisted by the pangs of conscience, this stranger did not cut a very noble figure, nor did he seem proud of his mission there. He nervously twisted a fold of his cloak between his fingers as those present looked on him with secret contempt.

"You are Judas Iscariot?"

"Yes."

"Is it true that you are one of the followers of the Nazarene, the false Messias, Jesus?"

"It is true."

Judas was uneasy. Were they going to hold it against him that he had been so long a follower of Jesus? Hurriedly, he cried out in a hoarse voice, "How much will you pay me to deliver Him to you?"

A shiver of excitement ran through the room. This time it

looked as if Jesus would be trapped. The bargain was struck for thirty pieces of silver in Jewish money, about what it would cost to buy a man's suit today. Not a great reward, really, for such a crime. The money was counted out. They arranged the details by which Judas would lead the servants of the Sanhedrin to the place where they could find Jesus alone. Everything was now settled, and the trap was ready to close on the Messias. Judas departed into the night and as he hastened along the steep and narrow streets he could hear tinkling in his pocket the coins that were the price of his treason.

XVI

The Last Supper

BEFORE THE FEAST, Jesus had said to His disciples, "I have longed to eat this Pascal meal with you. It is the last which we shall share until we are all reunited in heaven. Go, then, and make ready for the feast." It was because of these words that on Thursday, which we now call Holy Thursday, Peter and John went ahead of the others into Jerusalem, to the upper quarter of the town, to prepare for the ceremony.

A friend of the Master was only too happy to place at their disposal a room on the first story of his house, one of those huge rooms which the Jews called "cenacles." There the two Apostles arranged a long table surrounded by couches so that the guests might recline, and on the floor heavy carpets were placed. The Pascal lamb was bought, the ceremonial herbs and sauces prepared, and the wine jars set out. When Jesus and the other disciples arrived at nightfall, everything was ready and the ceremonies began.

To the Jews, the Passover was a time for rejoicing. Did it not commemorate a great favor conferred by God on their fathers? And so all through the meal they lifted their cups toward heaven and sang psalms in honor of the Lord, the Most High and Merciful God. "Praise the Lord, all ye nations; praise Him, all ye people. For His mercy is infinite and His trust endures forever." But Jesus intended that at this meal which was to be His last on earth He would teach His friends one all-important lesson. For this reason, instead of following the familiar Jewish ritual of hymns and canticles, He performed several new and unfamiliar rites.

First of all, just as the meal was about to begin, Jesus left the table, took off His outer robe and wrapped about His waist a towel. Then He poured water into a basin and proceeded to wash the feet of His disciples, afterward drying them with the towel—as all the supper guests were reclining on couches in the Eastern fashion it was possible for Him to do this without disturbing them.

When, however, He came to Simon Peter, the latter protested, "Lord, do *you* wash *my* feet?" For Peter felt himself unworthy of this unexpected honor.

Jesus replied, "You do not know now what I am doing, but you will know later."

"No, no," cried the Apostle. "You shall never wash my feet."

"If I do not wash you, you will have no part with Me in heaven," said Jesus.

"Lord, if that be so, not only my feet, but my hands and my head as well."

When Jesus had made the round of the table, washing the feet of each disciple in turn, He saw their surprise and exclaimed, "Do you know what I have done to you? You call me Master and Lord, and you say well, for so I am. If then I, being your Master and Lord, have made this gesture of humility, it is to teach you to be humble in your dealings with one another."

What a lesson there is for us in this: never to give way to pride, to be humble of heart and to serve our neighbors as Jesus served His friends. Such was one of the last lessons that Jesus taught before He departed. It is the reason why to this very day you see holy men and women, for example the Little Sisters of the Poor, devoting their whole lives to the care of the poor and unfortunate out of humility and for the love of God.

Christ now came back to His place at the table. The meal began. Earthenware lamps had been lighted overhead; outside it was already dark.

At one end of the table Judas held himself aloof. In contrast to the rest, who were enjoying the feast, he sat with his face convulsed by rage and mental agony. He had given his word that this very night he would lead the guards against his Master, and he dared not look Jesus in the face. Moreover, because of certain words uttered by Jesus, he was convinced that his infamy was known. For instance, while He was washing the disciples' feet, Jesus had murmured, "You are clean, but not all." In the course of the meal Jesus had gone still further and had expressly stated, "One of you shall betray me." Aghast and horrified, the Apostles one after another began to ask Jesus, "Is it I, Lord?" When it came to Judas' turn he had asked, "Is it I?" Just think of how the penetrating and all-seeing gaze of the Master fixed itself on him. Jesus barely whispered four little words but they went to the very depths of Judas' somber soul, "Thou hast said it." Even now, there was time for him to repent, to turn back. If, even now, he had begged Jesus to forgive him, the Master would have opened His arms and heart to him and shown him mercy. But it was not to be.

Judas arose and made for the door. As he went, Jesus called out to him, "What you do, do quickly."

None of the other Apostles understood what was going on. As Judas was the holder of their common purse, they supposed that Jesus had sent him out to buy something for the feast. Judas hurried off into the night, and the door of the supper room closed behind him.

Now the meal was drawing to an end. The Apostles who had paid no heed to the incident of Judas' departure were in good spirits because of the festival they had shared with their friend and Master. They gave no thought to what He had so recently told them—that this meal, this supper, would be the last one of His life on earth.

Suddenly, with a gesture, Jesus called for silence. Then He took bread, gave thanks to God, blessed the bread, broke it and gave a fragment to each, saying, "Take ye and eat; this is My Body, which shall be delivered for you."

Then, in similar manner, He took a cup of wine, gave thanks

to God, blessed the wine and offered it to the Apostles saying, "Drink ye all of this. This is My Blood of the new testament, which shall be shed for many, to the remission of sins."

Jesus ended by saying, "Do this in commemoration of Me."

We know these words well, for every Sunday at Mass, just before the elevation, the priest pronounces them over the bread and wine thus changing that bread and wine into the very Flesh and Blood of Christ. It is "in commemoration of Him" and in obedience to His command that priests, for nineteen hundred years, have celebrated the Mass. The Mass is an exact reproduction of the mysterious ceremony of the Last Supper. Exactly as the Apostles received the body and blood of Christ on the evening of that first Holy

Thursday, so do we receive Him when we go to Holy Communion. So was instituted the greatest of the Sacraments (your catechism tells you the exact meaning of the word): the Holy Eucharist, which enables the humblest and poorest of Christians to partake of Christ according to His promise.

Now, at last, the Apostles were able to understand the true meaning of the words which Jesus had spoken many months previously, "I am the Bread of Life." The Bread of Life, yes, from now on they would have this. Perhaps even now they did not quite realize the meaning of the words, "This is My Body. This is My Blood," but before long, when the sacrifice had been completed, when Jesus had willed to give His life for men, everything would be made clear to them. They would understand, as we understand, that in these fragments of bread and drops of wine consecrated by the words of Christ, every one of us possesses the Christ who offers His life for each and every one of us.

When their repast was finished, the company, as was the Jewish custom, remained in the supper room to finish the evening there. None of them had any wish to leave the Master's side, so happy were they made by His mere presence. Some of the things He had said had made them vaguely uneasy, and because of this they were all the more anxious to keep close to Him and to listen to every word He uttered. And Jesus continued to speak to them in a simple and loving way, and what He said contained some important lessons.

"Little children, I will be with you for only a little longer." At these words everyone was disturbed and asked Jesus to state more definitely what He meant. Were they in any immediate danger? If so, they were prepared to resist their enemies, to fight if necessary. "Lord," cried Peter, "I am willing to go with you both to prison, and to death." Jesus answered him gently, with pitying humor, "Ah, Peter, this very night, before the cock crows twice, you will deny me thrice." For Jesus knew well the weakness of human nature, so ready with words, so hesitant in deeds.

He continued, "I am the way and the truth and the life. No man can come to the Father, but by Me." By this Jesus meant that henceforth man could win heaven only by following the law of Christ. Again Jesus reminded them of the first of all His commandments: "Love one another, as I have loved you."

Then He continued in a graver tone, "Soon I will leave you, for I will leave the world and return to My Father, but you will see My glory, the glory of the Son of God. As for you, My friends, soon it will be your turn to suffer for your faith in Me. They will drive you out of the synagogues, persecute and even kill you. But have courage, I have conquered the world and with My help you also will conquer it. I will not leave you orphans. Remember always—the greatest love a man can show is that he should lay down his life for his friends."

How moving are these words in their simplicity and beauty. In His last hours, Jesus, who is about to die and who knows it, thinks only of His friends and of mankind. For them He came into the world in order to bring hope and consolation. So beautifully did Jesus speak on this occasion that St. John has set down carefully in his Gospel every word He uttered. And when all was ended and it was time to leave the supper room, Jesus raised His head and spoke one final prayer to His Father.

"Father," He prayed, "the time has come. I pray to You for these men whom Thou hast given Me. I am remaining in this world no longer but they remain in the world, so watch over them, Heavenly Father, and grant that they may have My joy in full measure. I make this prayer not merely for these eleven men with Me, but for all men who believe in Me, that they all may be one with Me in the place to which I go. I pray that the love which You have given Me be given to them also and that I too may be one with them."

When Jesus and His Apostles left the house, darkness had long since fallen and under the Paschal moon Jerusalem slept in the clear warm air of the April night. It was too late for the followers to return to Bethany and so, as it was such a warm night, they settled down in the open air in an olive grove called Gethsemani, which means "oil press" (see plan at end of book). The grove belonged to one of the Master's friends, possibly the parents of young Mark, the future Evangelist. The rippling waters of the brook Cedron sang among the rocks. From the high walls of the city there echoed the calls of the Roman sentinels one to another.

"Sit down here," Jesus told His disciples, "while I go a little further to pray. And you also pray and pray much, for it is the hour when the powers of darkness gather around."

Jesus fell on His knees among the olive trees a little apart from the others and began to pray. He had said to Peter, James and John, "My soul is sorrowful even unto death." And so began what is perhaps the most heart-rending scene in the whole Gospel, "the Agony in the Garden." Jesus was the Son of God, the Messias, the Almighty, but at the same time He was a man. He knew in advance the dreadful trials that awaited Him. Although He was God, His human nature was overwhelmed. And He was alone, terribly alone, for some yards away from Him the exhausted Apostles had fallen asleep, unable to keep vigil with their Master.

In an agonized voice Jesus called on His Father, "Father, if it be possible, let this chalice pass from Me." He begged not to be forced to drain to the dregs this bitter cup of suffering and torture. As He prayed, sweat, like great drops of blood, poured from His ravaged countenance. But He continued, "My Father, if this chalice may not pass away but I must drink it, Thy will be done." Mark well what Christ said even in this moment when His human body shrank and trembled in horror at what was to come. "Thy will be done." So did Jesus offer Himself as a victim, and so pleasing were His words to His Father that angels hastened to comfort Him.

It was at this moment that the sound of trampling footsteps and the clash of weapons resounded from the stony road. What was the meaning of the blaze of torches, and why were these Temple guards and servants, armed with swords and clubs, approaching from the town?

XVII

The Passion of Our Lord: The Mock Trial

WE NOW COME to the most dramatic chapter of the whole Gospel narrative, so moving that it tears at our heart-strings and so pitiful that it fills our eyes with tears. The word "Passion" means suffering or torture, and it is only too true that on this last day of His life, the sufferings and tortures inflicted on Jesus were almost inconceivable. From the moment when in the Garden of Olives His mental agony caused Him to sweat blood, to that when He gave up His soul to the Father, He was to suffer sixteen or seventeen hours of blows, outrage, ceaseless questioning and torture. We could but pity anyone, no matter what he had done, who had to undergo such suffering. But when we realize that the victim was the most gentle and generous soul that ever lived, the man whose great message to men was "Love one another," we are struck dumb with horror and feel that we must weep and pray.

The High Priest's troop had now reached the entrance to the Garden of Gethsemani. It was made up of Temple servants carrying lanterns and torches and with them were guards armed with swords and clubs. Judas had told them, "Whoever I shall kiss, that is He." You can imagine the excitement as the guards scattered through the olive trees, while the rudely-awakened Apostles huddled together uncertainly. Jesus alone remained motionless and calm in the midst of the tumult. The traitor approached Him and pretended to embrace Him. "So, Judas," said Christ in a low voice, "you betray Me with a kiss." We can still hear the terrible reproach in these words. Then Jesus approached the soldiers and asked them, "Whom do you seek?" and the reply was, "Jesus of Nazareth." "I am He," said Jesus. "Do not harm My friends. I will not resist you."

It was only at this moment that Peter became aware of what was going on. Leaping up, he drew his sword and struck one of the Temple servants, a man called Malchus, cutting off his ear. On seeing this, Jesus said to Peter, "Put back your sword. Do you not know that if I so wished it, God would send legions of angels to defend Me?" Touching Malchus' head, He healed the wound and then gave Himself into the hands of the soldiers. Overcome by what had happened, His disciples scattered and fled into the night.

Through the alleys and stairways of the city His escort pushed and dragged Jesus to the palace of the High Priest Caiphas. It was Caiphas who had presided at the night meetings of the plotters who had decided upon Jesus' destruction. He was the religious leader of the Jewish community but he had no right to question Jesus at night, for it was the law that legal trials could take place only in broad light of day. In spite of this, Caiphas was so impatient to see this man now at his mercy, that he caused Jesus to be brought before him at once and began to question Him on His teaching.

"I have never hidden Myself or spoken in secret," replied Jesus. "Ask those who have listened to Me and they will tell you what I teach."

The reply was so apt that Caiphas could not refrain from a gesture of anger, whereupon one of his servants promptly gave Jesus a blow—again a breach of the law which made it illegal to strike a prisoner. Other questions by the High Priest received equally apt replies from Christ.

Then Caiphas put a crucial question, "I abjure You, tell us whether You are the Messias, the Son of God?"

Jesus knew perfectly well that this question was intended to bring about His downfall. But the time had come for Him to reveal His identity to the whole world, so He said, "Thou hast said it. I am the Messias. And I say to you, that one day you will see the Son of Man seated at the right hand of the Father, and coming in the clouds of heaven."

Hearing this, Caiphas cried out and tore his garments, calling on those present to bear witness to what he pretended to consider a horrible blasphemy. "This man has called Himself the Son of God. He has blasphemed; what further need have we of witnesses? What say you?"

All of those present screamed out, "He deserves death."

While this preliminary inquiry was being held an unhappy incident took place in the courtyard of Caiphas' palace. The night being cool, a crowd of Temple attendants, guards and servants had gathered around a fire, discussing the arrest of Jesus. Some of the Apostles had tried to follow Jesus, mingling with the various groups. Among them was Peter, seeking news of the Master. A maidservant recognized him, and pointed him out, saying, "You were one of those with Jesus of Nazareth." Fear gripped Peter's heart and he trembled at the thought of what might happen if he were recognized. No, no, he protested: he never knew the Man, he even swore it. As he spoke a cock crowed in the night, but Peter was too excited to notice it.

An hour passed and Peter was again back in the courtyard, seeking news and asking questions. His Galilean accent, however, was strange to Judean ears and again he was accused. "Surely you are one of them," they cried out again. "Your accent betrays you as a Galilean." To make matters worse one of the Temple servants added, "I myself saw you with Jesus in the Garden of Olives." Thus cornered and trembling with fear, the unhappy Peter gave way, vowing and protesting over and over again, "I know not this Man of whom you speak. I never even saw Him." At this moment the cock crowed for the second time. Peter heard it and trembled. He remembered Christ's words and was bitterly ashamed of his cowardice. At the first threat of danger he had abandoned his Master! Now as he bowed his head, looking to right and left for some way of escape, Jesus appeared on the threshold of the palace, surrounded by guards. And His all-seeing gaze pierced the soul of the unhappy Peter to its very depths.

Jesus had been left to the mercies of His guard of soldiers and lackeys until the night was over. These decided to have some sport with this prisoner whom their leaders considered as a blasphemer. What followed was hour upon hour of shame, insult and outrage for Jesus. They blindfolded Him and one after another struck Him cruel blows, jeering at Him, "Come now, O Messias, You who know everything; tell us who has struck You." They spat in His face and subjected Him to every brutality that their minds could imagine. Jesus suffered in silence. Motionless, He prayed from the bottom of His heart, offering all the insults, the blows, the pain inflicted on Him in reparation for men's sins of pride and He begged God to forgive them.

At last another day dawned. During the night, Caiphas had sent word to all the members of the Sanhedrin, notifying them that their council would meet on an urgent matter. The members knew well what was afoot and were determined to miss nothing of the affair. So as the first light broke over the hills, Jesus was brought to the nearby Temple chamber where the Sanhedrin sat in readiness to pass judgment on Him. He appeared before His judges worn out after a sleepless night, His face covered with grime and sweat.

The Sanhedrin was the highest Jewish authority, the Council of Seventy instituted by Moses. It was both the government and the supreme court of the community. Before it appeared all those accused of offenses against the Law of Moses, and the sacred Scriptures contained numerous regulations for the protection of accused persons, insuring the absolute justice of their trial. But for Jesus none of the legal forms was observed. His fate, as we all know, had already been decided by the plotters at their meetings at Caiphas' country house and this final appearance before the San-hedrin was nothing but a legal farce. Once again He was asked if He claimed to be the Messias and once again He was accused of blasphemy. . . .

When, surrounded by guards, Jesus emerged from the council chamber, the whisper ran like wildfire from mouth to mouth, "Death! The Sanhedrin has condemned Him to death."

Among the crowd which had gathered out of curiosity, there was one man who appeared to be greatly stricken by the verdict; it was Judas the traitor. What then had he thought would happen when he betrayed his Master? Did he really believe that Jesus' enemies would be content to arrest Him and put Him in prison? He had not thought that all this would end in such tragedy. Re-morse now struck his somber heart. He had not wanted this to happen. He did not want it! . . . Taking his thirty pieces of silver, he went and threw them at the feet of the priests and doctors of the Law, crying out, "I have sinned in betraying an innocent man." He was too late, for the only reply was, "What is that to us; look you to it." Deserted by everyone and despised even by those who had used him as a tool, the miserable wretch was left alone with his conscience.

And yet, Judas could have saved himself if even now he had knelt down and implored mercy from God. If he had sought out Jesus and begged forgiveness, the Master, always so ready to for-give humanity its worst human faults, would not have refused him. But it was not to be, for now the devil had complete mastery over Judas' soul. He would not allow him to repent. So Judas fled away from the city. In a deserted place he found a withered tree. Throw-ing a rope over one of its branches, he ended his life by hanging himself from it.

Jesus had been condemned to death by the council of the Jewish community, but they had no authority to execute Him. Since they had occupied Judea and made themselves responsible for maintaining order there, the Romans had forbidden the Jews to put anyone to death without their consent. So the next step for the Sanhedrin was to approach the Roman procurator, Pontius Pilate, and induce him to agree to Jesus' death.

Now Pontius Pilate was not a wicked man and personally he had nothing against Jesus. He was not, however, a man of strong character. He was above all an official, anxious at all costs to avoid trouble with the higher authorities of the Imperial government. Hearing the clamor of the crowd and the demonstration staged by the Sanhedrin, he emerged from his dwelling in the Antonia Palace beside the Temple (see plan). "What charge do you make against this man?" he asked. What were they going to reply? If they told the truth, that Jesus was accused of claiming to be the Son of God, Pilate, a Roman, would not look upon this as a very grave matter. Accordingly they resorted to lies and a series of new charges. "He is a disturber of the peace, forbidding the people to pay tribute to Caesar. He claims for Himself the title of King." All this was false, abominably false, but that did not disturb Pilate greatly.

He ordered Jesus to be brought before him and asked Him, "Is it true that You claim to be King of the Jews?"

"My kingdom is not of this world," replied Jesus. "If it were, My servants would not have allowed Me to be delivered to the Jews. I came into the world to give testimony to the truth. It is those who know the truth who shall enter into My kingdom."

Pilate shrugged his shoulders at this, for the cynical Roman did not understand such language. "What is truth?" he asked. Then, turning to the crowd, he declared, "I find no evil in this man." Evidently he thought that Jesus was a poor simpleton, not quite right in His mind. But the maddened crowd kept shouting, "Death to the Galilean!"

The word "Galilean" showed Pilate a possible way out of his difficulty. Jesus was a Galilean? Well then, why not send Him for judgment to Herod Antipas, the ruler of Galilee? It so happened that Herod, the husband of Herodias, the murderer of John the Baptist, was in Jerusalem at the time. So Jesus was led out again through the streets of the city, surrounded by guards and followed by a howling mob.

Herod was greatly interested. Here then was the Jesus he had heard so much about. Perhaps He would say something extraordinary or would work some miracle. He questioned Him, but Jesus was silent. He would not speak to this petty tyrant whose hands were red with the blood of John the Baptist. Finally Herod gave up and was about to send Jesus back to Pilate when an amusing idea struck him. Jesus said He was a king; what a joke it would be to dress Him up as one. Herod sent for a really royal robe and placed it on Jesus, for he felt sure that Pilate would be amused by this. Besides it would annoy those Jews of Jerusalem for whom Herod had little liking. So Jesus was sent forth again dressed in a splendid white tunic that only emphasized the paleness of His drawn and weary face.

Once again Jesus was before Pilate and the latter did not know what to do. Once more he told the priests and lawyers, "He is guilty of no crime: I have questioned Him myself and find no evil in Him. No, nor has Herod, who has sent Him back to me. You say He has caused some disturbance? Well, for this I will have Him scourged, and then I will release Him."

The crowd howled its protests at this decision, and Pilate became uneasy, for the last thing he wanted was to provoke a riot that would have to be put down by force. Rome would not like that at all, so Pilate sought another way out of his difficulty. It was the custom every year at Passover time to grant a pardon to some criminal condemned to death, and Pilate thought to save Jesus in this manner. Turning to the crowd he said to them, "Which man would you like me to pardon—Jesus who calls Himself King of the Jews, or the highwayman Barabbas who is under sentence of death for his crimes?" Pilate was convinced that the crowd would cry out the name of Jesus rather than that of Barabbas the criminal. But he was wrong. Stirred up to a state of frenzy by their leaders, the people yelled, "Release Barabbas! Away with Jesus!"

Pilate was at his wits' end to know what to do, particularly as just at this moment his wife sent him a message: "Last night I dreamed about this man who is before you. He is innocent. Do not mix in this affair." But what could he do with this maddened crowd which kept shrieking, "Crucify Him, crucify Him!" It looked as though there might be an uprising at any moment.

Pilate had one last idea, an idea that perhaps was intended for the best but which inflicted new tortures on Jesus. He had said that he would punish Jesus, and now he gave the order to have Him scourged, believing perhaps that the crowd would take pity on Jesus when they saw His pitiable state after He had been beaten. So the torture commenced and it was horrible. The whips whistled through the air, tearing the skin from Jesus' back, so that in a moment He had fallen at the foot of a column, an inert mass of bleeding flesh.

When this awful scene was over, the soldiers lifted Him up and threw Him on a stone bench. They were quite pitiless to their tortured victim, indeed He was a figure of mockery to them. This sorry-looking King of the Jews who made no attempt to defend Himself! They made game of Him and decided that since He was a king He had better have a crown. They broke off branches from a long-thorned acacia tree, and wove them into a crown which they forced down on Jesus' head so that the thorns sank deep into His flesh. They threw a red cloak over His shoulders, and one by one they knelt in mockery before Him crying out, "Hail, King of the Jews!"

We may well ask ourselves how Christ tolerated this hideous

mockery, why He did not call upon His heavenly Father to destroy this horrible crew of ruffians who were tormenting Him? It was because He wished to teach us all this great lesson: it is when we are suffering from injustice, ill treatment and the contempt of others that we come closest to the heart of God.

Finally it was over. Hours had passed, and every moment of them had been one of torture for Jesus, when Pilate came near to Him and ordered his men to lift Him up and show Him to the crowd. *"Ecce homo,"* he cried, which means "Behold the man." Surely He was such a wretched sight, so obviously at the end of His strength, that the hardest heart could but feel pity for Him. But no, the crowd redoubled its shouts of "Crucify Him, crucify Him." Then, as Pilate still hesitated, they threatened him, yelling, "If you release this Man, you are not the Emperor's friend. Jesus wishes to make Himself king against Caesar." It was this final falsehood that decided Pilate. He feared that these Jews might denounce him to Rome for having protected a rebel. So because he lacked the courage to administer justice, and although he knew that Jesus was innocent, he gave up all attempt to protect Him.

He sent for a basin of water and washed his hands in full sight of the crowd, saying, "I wash my hands of the blood of this innocent man. I will not be responsible." As though this statement could relieve him of all responsibility for the crime about to be committed. . . . He then made a sign to his soldiers to deliver their victim to the Jews. So ended the tragic farce of this unbelievable "trial."

XVIII

The End of Christ's Passion: His Death on the Cross

AND NOW A FEARFUL and pitiful procession made its way through the streets of Jerusalem. First of all came a centurion, leading a company of Roman soldiers. They were followed by a man bearing a placard with the inscription written in Latin, Greek and Hebrew: "Jesus of Nazareth, King of the Jews." (Pilate himself had written the last four words in order to humiliate the Jews and to place all the responsibility on them.) Next in the procession came the priests of the Temple and members of the Sanhedrin, determined to be present at the death of the Man they hated. Then followed a rabble of the idle and curious, morbidly anxious to watch the torture of a fellow being. Christ's friends were there too, beside themselves with grief but powerless to help. Finally, Jesus Himself. . . .

He was at the end of His strength: panting, His face streaming with cold sweat, His forehead torn with thorns. He moved slowly, totteringly, seemingly on the verge of collapse, surrounded by brutal guards who struck Him at every false step. According to the rule which laid down this added punishment, He carried His cross, and for a man so worn out with pain and ill-treatment, the burden was all but intolerable. It was not far from Pilate's stronghold to the place of execution (see plan at end of this book), between five hundred and six hundred yards, but this distance was made up of alleyways broken by steps to be mounted and descended, so that for Jesus the way was a terrible one. Once, twice, and again a third time, His foot slipped on an uneven pave-

ment stone or on a step; He fell under the weight of the cross and its heavy beams struck Him as He fell. Each time it took Him a little longer to rise, so that finally the soldiers feared that He might die of exhaustion on the way. So they ordered a passer-by, a man called Simon of Cyrene, to help Him to carry His load.

But was there no one ready to come to Jesus' aid as He suffered His unmerited torture? Of all the vast crowds that had hailed His triumph on the previous Sunday, was there none to raise a hand in His defense? Not one. His disciples, terrified since His arrest, had fled for safety and hidden themselves in the lower quarter of the town among the tombs of Zachary and Absalom. The onlookers who had cheered Him so enthusiastically the previous Sunday had lost all interest in Him in His hour of defeat. In the whole crowd there were only a few weeping women who had the courage even to wipe the face of the poor victim, and to these Jesus spoke a few consoling words. But apart from them, He was deserted by all. The Messias went to His doom utterly alone, betrayed by nearly all mankind—the mankind He had loved so well.

The place of public execution to which Jesus was being led was just beyond the city walls on a piece of wasteland scattered with tombs (see plan). It was called "Golgotha" and "Calvary" from the Aramaic and Latin words meaning a bare mound, and was a rocky hillock overlooking the road which led from Jerusalem to the sea. A cross placed on the top of this mound would be visible from all directions, and the condemned man would be an object of fear and horror to all passers-by. Today this mound is covered over by an immense and splendid basilica built by the Crusaders in the twelfth century when, under Godfrey de Bouillon, they captured the city (as you have no doubt read in your history classes at school). Jesus and His escort passed through the city gates and halted when they reached Calvary.

I only wish that we could quickly turn over the next few pages of the Gospel, so as not to have to read the full story of the cruelty and injustice contained in the three words, "Jesus was crucified." We repeat this simple phrase every time we recite the Apostles' Creed, but I wonder if we ever really reflect on the horror and agony that it implied for the Man who suffered this cruel ordeal.

Death on the cross was a revolting form of torture. According to the Roman writer Cicero, "the most terrible of all tortures"; it was reserved for rebellious slaves and those guilty of the most abominable crimes. With his hands nailed or tied by ropes to the crosspiece, the condemned man was left to hang for interminable hours. It is on record that in certain cases it took three days for death to come to his relief. The victim's body, dragging on the muscles, became contracted and stiff, while he was suffocated by unbearable pain in his chest. His throat and stomach burned with thirst and his whole being was sunk in a sea of agony.

This then was the death decreed for Jesus, the Sinless One, the purest and holiest being who ever lived on earth. The very thought of this injustice is so horrible that our minds and consciences revolt from it. Christian writers have described the cross as "a scandal" and they are right. But we must always remember that the terrible tragedy and suffering of His crucifixion were willed by Christ Himself. Had He wished it, He whom the winds and waves obeyed, before whom the powers of darkness had fled, He who had raised Lazarus from the dead, could have stepped down from the cross and destroyed His enemies with a single word. We see therefore that the cross was not merely a scandal; it was also a mystery, that supreme mystery of Jesus' love for mankind that is called the "Redemption."

In what does this mystery consist? In this: that Jesus, the Son of God, the Perfect One, came to earth in order to bring salvation to men. We are all sinners, wicked, violent, unbelieving and rebellious, and because our sins are an unceasing offense against Divine justice, we are punished for them. Our hearts are filled with unhappiness and misery, we suffer in body and in mind and in the end we die. Now when Jesus offered up His life on the cross, His intention was that He, the Sinless One, the purest of the pure, should take on Himself the burden of all the sins of mankind and say to His heavenly Father, "Father, it is I, and I alone, who will bear the punishment that Your justice has decreed for the countless sins of mankind. I accept such suffering as no man has ever been called upon to bear; I accept death provided You will forgive men. I know well all that they are, I know all their sins, but in My name, in the name of the tortures I am suffering, I implore you to have pity on these poor men. Restore to them the divine life they have lost through sin. Almighty Father, forgive them in the name of My cross."

And that was why Jesus submitted to all the injustice, the cruelty and the horror of His crucifixion. You remember that He had spoken these words: "Greater love than this no man has, that he should lay down his life for his friends." By His death on the cross in expiation of our sins, the Master gave this final proof of His infinite love for us.

It was about noon on Friday the 7th day of April in the year 30 when, by dint of much hauling on ropes and timbers and with shouted orders, that the executioners finally erected the cross on Calvary. In fact, there were three crosses, because it had been decided to execute two criminals at the same time as Jesus. This was done as an added humiliation to the self-styled Messias, to show that in the eyes of the law there was no difference between Him and these petty thieves. So much, said the Pharisees, for His claim to be the Son of God!

But scarcely was the cross in position, its grim arms outlined against the sky, when some very strange happenings took place. A dense black cloud of unnatural appearance appeared over Jerusalem and the surrounding district, casting deep shadows where no shadows should be at noon on a clear spring day. Rumblings came from the earth as though an earthquake were about to take place. Soon the rumor spread that the tombs of the dead had opened, and that the dead had been seen to appear. It seems as though the very laws of nature reeled before the horror that was about to take place.

Crowds moved uneasily about the crosses on Calvary. Visitors who had come to Jerusalem for the festival wanted to see for themselves what was going on. And of course the members of the Sanhedrin and all the rest of Jesus' enemies were there to gloat over their victim and to jeer at Him. "You who call Yourself the Son of God, now is the time to show Your power. Come down from Your cross if You can!" From the height of the cross Jesus looked down upon these craven people He could have destroyed with only a word; but not a syllable of anger, vengeance or even protest fell from Him. On the contrary: from lips twisted in agony He was heard to murmur, "Father, forgive them, for they know not what they do."

To one side, near the foot of the cross, the soldiers and the executioners awaited the end, passing the time with a game of dice. They had divided the garments of the condemned men as was their right, for the law allowed them this as their fee. But as Jesus' tunic was a single seamless piece, they could not divide it and so they cast lots to see to whom it should belong.

The minutes dragged by slowly, so very slowly, until suddenly the heavy silence was broken by the snarling voice of one of the thieves who was dying in Jesus' company. Mad with pain, he screamed and shouted. Then he cried out to Jesus, "If you are the Messias, save Yourself and us." But from the third cross another voice was raised, "Have you, then, no fear of the Lord, that you speak so? We suffer the just punishment of our crimes, but this Man has done no evil." Then this poor wretch, his soul filled with faith, called on Jesus, "Lord, remember me when You have come into Your kingdom." Moved by his words, Jesus replied, "I promise you that on this very day you shall be with Me in Paradise." By accepting death as the just punishment of his sins and by showing his complete faith in Christ, this poor penitent thief had touched the heart of God.

Meanwhile, braving the mysterious darkness that enshrouded the cross, another group of people drew near. In it were John the beloved disciple, Mary of Bethany, the old friend of happy bygone days, and perhaps also the sad figure of that other woman who had poured perfume over the Master's feet. Above all, here was Mary the Blessed Virgin, the Mother of Jesus, who had found in her great heart the courage to follow her Son's ordeal to the bitter end. There they were rooted to the earth, their gaze fixed on that beloved head that now was bowed in agony. Jesus saw them and their presence brought some consolation to His poor human heart. To His mother, He said, "Behold thy son," and He indicated John. While to John He said, "Behold thy mother."

These were almost the last words uttered by Jesus. Time dragged on and in the terrible silence He was heard to whisper, "I thirst." A soldier who was standing near took pity on Him and dipping a sponge in a mixture of water and vinegar, he placed it on the point of a lance and raised it to Jesus' lips.

All the while the shadows grew deeper, and the sinister rumblings of the earth continued as though nature itself were struggling in its death throes. At about three o'clock in the afternoon, Jesus called aloud to His heavenly Father, "Into Thy hands I commend My spirit." And that was all. His head fell forward on His breast and He breathed His last.

At this moment in the Temple the great veil that covered the entrance to the Holy of Holies was suddenly torn apart. . . .

The ceremonies of the Passover were due to begin. It was only a matter of hours before the three blasts of the sacred trumpets would be heard and the High Priest would ascend the steps leading to the Holy of Holies. But now the people of the Temple and of the Sanhedrin, who had been certain of their complete victory over Jesus, began to grow excited. This affair must be brought to an end without any further delay, and so they sent soldiers to make quitet sure that the three victims were dead; if not, they were to finish them off by breaking their limbs. In Jesus' case, this was not necessary, for He was already dead. To make quite sure of this a soldier drove his lance into Jesus' side and blood and water gushed forth from the open wound. Now they could report back to Pilate and reassure the priests and Pharisees that the object of their hatred was indeed dead, and ready for burial.

What was needed was a grave, and that quickly. For it was absolutely forbidden by the law to leave the body of an executed man exposed during festival time. And so Jesus' friends were allowed to take His body down from the cross. This they did, lovingly and tenderly. Mary, the heroic mother, received the body in her arms and for a moment pressed the beloved head to her breast as she had so often done when He was a little child. Lovingly the body was washed, and so far as possible all traces of its horrible injuries removed. Time was pressing (for everything must be finished before nightfall when the Sabbath began) and so hurriedly the body was anointed with fragrant oils and wrapped in bands of white linen.

Some fifty yards from the cross there was a new tomb which had never been used. It belonged to one of Jesus' followers, Joseph of Arimathea. He gladly placed it at the disposal of the friends of the Crucified Christ. There, on a stone bench at the end of the burial chamber, the body was laid, the head supported by a small cushion. Then the burial party withdrew. A heavy stone was placed in position at the mouth of the passage leading to the tomb. All was over. Was this truly the end of Jesus?

XIX
The Resurrection

B UT NO, this was far from being the end of Jesus! Who should
have known this better than the Apostles, those privileged
few who over and over again had heard Him say, "On the third
day I will rise again"? Had they not seen His amazing victory
over death when He raised Lazarus from the tomb?

All the same it was hard for them to have faith in the future.
With their own eyes they had witnessed Jesus' defeat; they had
seen Him tortured and crucified, and with their own hands they
had laid His body in the tomb; everything seemed to prove that
their Master had been vanquished. And as they were only human,
it was pardonable for them to be heartbroken, terrified and overwhelmed by the disaster that had befallen them. Huddled together
in hiding near the cemetery, expecting in their turn to be arrested
at any moment, they kept going over and over again the terrible
events of the previous day. Jesus' death had taken all meaning out
of their lives and fearfully they asked each other what was going
to happen next.

As for Jesus' enemies, they were of course wild with triumph.
How easy it had been, after all, to get rid of this prophet, this self-
styled Messias, who for two years had such an enthusiastic following, who claimed to have worked such wondrous miracles, and
who was even said to have raised the dead to life. Not a hand had
been raised to defend Him, not a protest from His fanatical sup-
porters. In another week people would have forgotten all about
Him! Yet meanwhile it was well to be on the safe side: armed
guards had been placed near His tomb, for fear His disciples
would try to steal away His body and then claim that He had

risen from the dead. With the guards there, they could rest at ease, for assuredly without help Jesus of Nazareth could not come forth from His tomb.

It was then that there took place, on the third day—that is, on Sunday morning, exactly as Jesus had foretold—the most extraordinary event of the wonderful Gospel story. All four Evangelists have told us of it, and later one of the first leaders of the Christian Church, St. Paul, was rightly to exclaim, "If Christ be not risen again, then is our preaching vain, and your faith is also vain!" Christ rose as He had Himself foretold, to prove to the entire world and to all future generations of mankind that He was truly the Son of God, the Master of life and death. The resurrection of Christ is such an amazing event that we would not dare to believe it were it not for the proof the Gospels give us. It marks the greatest date in the entire history of mankind, and we commemorate it on Easter Sunday, that joyous feast with all its promise of life everlasting.

During these hours when the body of Jesus lay in the darkness of the tomb, where was His soul? As always, He was engaged on a mission of mercy. He had descended into limbo, the dark kingdom of the dead, where for countless centuries thousands of just souls had waited and hoped for the coming of the Saviour who would open to them the gates of the Kingdom of heaven. What a moment it must have been for these poor souls when Jesus appeared among them, to bring them in person the joyful tidings of their Redemption!

Sunday dawned, a beautiful spring morning, warm, sunny and loud with bird song. Day had scarcely broken when from the upper quarter of the town a group of women might have been seen hurrying along the hilly streets toward the Ephraim Gate. They bore heavy parcels on their shoulders or, as is the custom in the East, balanced on their heads. They were five or six in number, and several of them are already known to us. First among them was Mary Magdalen, she who had poured perfume over the feet of the living Jesus. Now she and her companions were carrying perfumes to anoint His dead body. Throughout the East it is the custom to surround the dead with sweet-smelling substances and drugs in order to prevent corruption. In Egypt, as you may remember, the dead were embalmed.

It was to perform this pious task that these women were making their way to Jesus' tomb on Sunday morning; on Friday there had not been time to place the aromatic perfumes in the tomb; and on Saturday, which was the Sabbath, all forms of labor were forbidden. The women hurried along, almost running in their excitement and distress. And as they went, they asked one another, "Who will roll back the stone from the door of the tomb? We will never be able to move such a weight ourselves."

When they arrived at the sepulcher, they cried out in wonder.
. . . It was open! The stone had been rolled away and the tomb
was empty. What had happened? The women were dumbfounded
and troubled. Suddenly they saw a shining figure seated near the
tomb. He appeared to be a young man, a warrior, and his garments shone like snow in the sun. Some yards away the soldiers
of the Sanhedrin guard lay stretched out motionless on the ground,
gazing with awe on this shining being. He was an angel, an angel
of God who had performed this miracle and moved from its groove
the great slab that could not be stirred by twenty ordinary men.
While the thunderstruck women gazed on the scene in silence the
angel spoke to them. "Why seek you the living among the dead?
He is not here, He is risen. Do you not remember what He told
you: that He would be delivered into the hands of His enemies,
and He would be crucified, but that on the third day He would
rise again. Now today this has happened. He is risen."

And now a change took place as grief gave way to joy. Swiftly
the faithful women ran to the place where they knew the Apostles were in hiding in order to bring the amazing news to them.
Not all of them went, however; one remained, Mary Magdalen,
whose love for Jesus was even greater than that of the others. She
had fallen on her knees, weeping and praying. She was troubled,
for she did not quite understand what had taken place. The guards
had all fled and she was alone. Then through her tears she saw
coming toward her someone she did not recognize; she thought it
was some workman or gardener of the cemetery. Suddenly she
heard the voice of the Master calling her by name: "Mary." She
raised her tearful face, overcome by joy and emotion. She could
only utter a word, a single word: "Master." She could say no more;
He was here, He had risen.

At this moment a clatter of footsteps could be heard coming
from the direction of the city gate. The Apostles arrived. At first
they had hesitated to believe the story brought by the women, but
finally, and still far from convinced, they agreed to come to Gol-

gotha to see for themselves. John, the youngest, who in his excitement had run all the way, came first. At his heels was Peter himself, the leader of the Apostles. They looked around them, hardly daring to believe the evidence of their own eyes. All the women had told them was true: the stone was rolled back, the tomb empty. Jesus' shroud lay on the ground. Everything had happened as the Divine Master had so often foretold. HE WAS RISEN.

Jesus remained on earth for forty days after his Resurrection, a second life which, while it resembled the first in many ways, was in others very different. He was to be seen both in Judea and in Galilee, again on the banks of the Lake of Tiberias, sharing meals with His disciples and talking to them exactly as of yore. On one occasion He even repeated the miracle of the draught of fishes which had marked the beginning of His public life, as if to emphasize to His friends that soon they must become fishers of men and draw into their nets countless thousands of human souls.

At the same time, many strange events took place during the forty days, and they proved that the risen Christ was something more than an ordinary human being. For instance, one evening the disciples were once more assembled in the Cenacle, the hall where, as you remember, they had taken part in the Last Supper. The doors had not merely been shut but barricaded, out of fear of the Jewish authorities. Suddenly Jesus appeared in their midst "without the door being opened." This was truly miraculous, and many such things occurred in the period that followed the Resurrection.

Indeed so many strange things happened that even some of Jesus' oldest friends hesitated to believe in all of them. For instance, the Apostle Thomas, who had not been present with the others on Easter Sunday morning, refused to believe in the Resurrection. When the others told him that they had actually seen the Master, he replied, "Until I see in His hands the marks of the nails and put my finger in the place of the nails, and until I put my hand into His side, I will not believe." But some little while later when Thomas was with the other Apostles in a room behind locked doors, suddenly Jesus appeared among them. He called Thomas, saying, "Put in your finger, and see My hands. And place your hands in the wound in My side. Do you believe now, Thomas?" Falling on his knees, overcome by love and wonder, the Apostle could only stammer out the words, "My Lord and My God!"

So passed these forty days of complete and utter happiness. His followers knew now beyond any shadow of doubt the truth of what Jesus had told them: He had triumphed over His enemies and He had conquered death itself. The future of His work was bright with the promise of victory. Instead of being discouraged and miserable, the hearts of Jesus' friends were aflame with zeal and confidence.

When, on several occasions during those forty days, Christ in the course of His final teaching told the disciples, "Going therefore, teach all nations, and fear not, for I shall be with you all days even to the end of the world," you can imagine the strength and confidence that filled their souls. From now on, nothing could stop them in their mission; their fervor would be proof against treachery or even violence. They were sure that Christ's work was everlasting, that it would conquer the world and survive time itself.

There is a great lesson for us to learn when we see the absolute faith that Jesus' Resurrection had aroused in the hearts of His followers. It is that every human soul can be sure that he will triumph over death and win life everlasting if only he loves and believes in Jesus from the depths of his heart.

This great truth is shown by a very simple but beautiful and consoling incident that occurred at this period. It shows clearly that Jesus intended for His Resurrection to bring hope to all men and to offer to the humblest of us the prospect of eternal happiness. Here is the story, which is known as "the meeting on the road to Emmaus."

On the evening of the Sunday following the Crucifixion, two men left Jerusalem by the road leading westward, making their way back to their native village of Emmaus (see map). They were simple, humble men and their hearts were heavy, for they had known and loved Jesus during His life. Now they believed Him dead and they grieved bitterly for Him.

They were sadly discussing the happenings of the previous Friday when they were joined by a fellow traveler who asked them why they were in such low spirits.

"Surely as you come from Jerusalem, you know what has happened there?" replied one of them.

"Well, what *has* happened?"

"Oh, that terrible affair of Jesus of Nazareth. He was a great prophet, a wonderfully good man, but the people's leaders condemned Him to death and crucified Him. We had really believed Him to be the Messias, the Saviour of Israel."

The second man added, "There is a rumor that this morning some women found His tomb empty and that angels appeared to them and said He had risen. But do you really believe that a man who is dead can come to life again?"

Then the stranger began to speak: "But have the Prophets not foretold all this? Did they not say that the Messias would die and rise again?" Quoting from the Scriptures, He explained at length all the prophecies. He spoke so beautifully and so interestingly that when they reached Emmaus, His new friends invited Him to stay and share a meal with them and He accepted. As they ate, the stranger continued to speak and His hosts felt an extraordinary feeling of well-being come over them. Their hearts became filled with happiness and confidence, so that their earlier gloom was completely driven away. . . .

Then, as He sat at table, their unknown friend took a piece of bread, broke it and raised it toward heaven while He uttered a prayer. It was a gesture they recognized and unmistakably, over-whelmed with happiness, they understood at last. . . . But before they could say a word, Jesus—for it was He—had disappeared. But from now on there would never again be sadness or uncertainty or uneasiness in the hearts of the two disciples of Emmaus, for before He disappeared the Master had filled their souls with happiness and with faith.

XX

The Church Founded by Jesus

AND NOW, my dear children, we come to the end of the story of our Lord Jesus Christ, as told to us in the four Gospels. Almost forty days had passed since the Resurrection and Jesus' teaching mission was completed. He knew that from now on, men could find salvation in the Good News He had brought them; by living in accordance with His teaching and by following His example, they could win for themselves the Kingdom of heaven and share with Him the happiness of life everlasting. He could hear His heavenly Father's voice calling Him back to reign with Him as Lord of the Universe.

He had directed His disciples to return to Jerusalem, that holiest of cities that so recently had been the scene of His Passion. No doubt He wished His final triumph to take place on the scene of His agony, and for the very city that had refused to recognize Him as the Messias to witness the supreme manifestation of His glory.

Jesus' last day on earth was warm and sunny, one of those May days which in Palestine proclaim the fact that summer is at hand. Followed by His friends, Jesus took the road they had so often traveled before, the road that leads through the valley of the Cedron toward the high hill facing the city—Mount Olivet. They climbed to the summit and there Jesus halted, while His disciples made a circle around Him for the last sight of Him that they would have on earth.

Turning His face toward the light, His hands raised to heaven, Jesus became rapt in prayer, in silent conversation with His Father. In deep silence the Apostles and the holy women watched Him as

they too poured out their hearts in prayer. Then suddenly they noticed that Jesus' feet were no longer touching the ground. It was as though the very power of His prayers were drawing Him away from earth toward heaven. Hardly realizing what was happening, the awe-stricken onlookers gazed at this mysterious scene. Above them Jesus lifted His arms in a final blessing. Higher and higher He rose, so that already He seemed no longer a part of this earth. A few moments later there was nothing, only an empty space where the Divine Master had stood. The Father had called back His Son, and the Ascension was over.

Rooted to the spot by amazement, the disciples kept their gaze fixed on the cloud in the heavens which now concealed the Master's form. Suddenly two shining angels appeared to them and said, "Men of Galilee, why stand you looking up to heaven? Do you not know that Jesus, who has just been taken from you, will return one day in like manner?" For, as you know, Christ had foretold His second coming and had said to the High Priest that one day He would return to earth in all His glory, accompanied by legions of angels; that this day would mark the end of the world and the day of judgment for all mankind. . . .

Jesus, however, did not desert mankind when He returned to His heavenly home. On the contrary, during the two years He had spent in teaching His doctrine, He, who knew and foresaw all things, had perfected an organization whose special mission it would be, after He had gone, to continue His work and to spread His Good Tidings throughout the world. This organization, founded by Jesus Christ Himself, is the Christian Church which, through all the centuries that have elapsed between His time and ours, has never ceased to fulfill the mission entrusted to her by her Master.

Who then were those people whom Jesus had called upon to be members of His Assembly (for we must remember that the word "Church" means the assembly of all the friends of Jesus)? His call was to all mankind, to every man, woman and child in the world. His message was intended not merely for the Jews, but for all nations of the world. Nor was it intended only for wise men and scholars; it was so worded that the simplest and youngest could understand it. Everyone who follows Jesus, everyone who has been baptized and humbly seeks forgiveness for his sins and proclaims his faith in Jesus as the Saviour and Redeemer of mankind, is therefore a Christian and a member of Christ's Church.

Jesus' teaching was intended not merely for His followers and friends, but for all those who until the end of time were to hear His words and follow His precepts. Do you remember the words He spoke during the Sermon on the Mount, His discourses to His disciples and His parables? In these are to be found the principles of the Christian Church—all of them. It is our duty as members of the Church to do our very best to live according to those principles—not always an easy task, for we are but men, and men have many faults.

To make it easier for us to follow His rule, Jesus has given us even more: He gave us the Sacraments, those spiritual aids that enable us to follow His example and to share in His divine life. Of all the Sacraments, the most important and the most wonderful is the Holy Eucharist, instituted by Him, as you remember, at the Last Supper. The Holy Eucharist is the "Bread of Life," unendingly consecrated and multipled by the Church according to Christ's mandate. It permits every Christian to receive within himself the divine strength of the Son of God.

Finally, Jesus gave a real organization to His Church, for He well knew the need of order and discipline in all human affairs. It was for this reason that He chose the leaders, the Apostles, to guide and direct the body of the faithful, and He entrusted to these Apostles the powers that He derived from God. At their head He placed Peter, whom He had named as His successor, to make known His Will when He would no longer be there.

How well all had been foreseen and divinely planned! And, as a final promise to those who would constitute His Church, the Master said, "Behold, I am with you all days, even to the end of the world." Although invisible to our eyes, Christ is ever present in the bosom of His Church; from heaven He directs and protects it. Never from the moment of His Ascension has He ceased to cherish the Church with His own unending love.

Let us now return to these first members of the Church, the Master's disciples, as they made their way down through the olive groves from the hilltop whence Jesus had ascended into heaven. There must have been grief in their hearts because the beloved Master was no longer with them, but this grief was mixed with a great happiness. Had He not made them partners in His work? Were they not henceforth to give testimony of Him on earth? They had been chosen by Him to spread the Good News and, when their earthly life was over, they would be joined to Him in heaven.

Peter, who had now taken over his role as leader, said to them, "Let us all return to the Cenacle where we gathered with the Master on the night before He died. Has He not told us that He will send the Holy Spirit to us to bring us the courage and strength for the task He has laid upon us?"

For ten days the Apostles stayed in the Cenacle, their time spent in prayer and reflection. The orders given by Jesus were precise: "Going therefore, teach all nations . . . you shall be My witnesses to the uttermost parts of the earth." Of course they must obey, but how? No doubt the principal subject of discussion in the Cenacle was the best method of carrying out the orders given to them. Should they go at once into the market places and the Temple courtyard and there proclaim Jesus as the Messias? In doing so would they not risk the anger of the Jewish authorities and their own arrest? Or did Jesus wish them to leave the Holy City and to preach His doctrine throughout the land and perhaps even outside of Palestine?

Exactly ten days after the Ascension they were still pondering these matters when a final miracle took place. It was on the feast of "Pentecost" which, among the Jews, commemorated the giving of the Tablets of the Law to Moses, that is, the greatest instance in ancient times of Divine Revelation to man.[1] Now an even more important revelation was about to be made. The disciples were gathered in prayer in the Cenacle, when suddenly there came from heaven the noise of a great wind, which filled the whole house. Then into the room itself there appeared tongues of fire which seemed to hover for a second, and then to settle on the head of each Apostle. At this moment each was filled with the spirit of God. All that had appeared to them hard to understand became marvelously clear. Now the way they were to act and to carry out the Master's orders became simple and definite. To their amazement, they quickly discovered that each of them could make himself understood in every language; no matter who listened to them, he heard their words in his own tongue. Finally, and this was perhaps the most important thing of all, each of the disciples was filled with courage to face all trials; he was ready to preach the Gospel to the farthest ends of the earth; from now on, none among them was to know fear.

This, then, was the final miracle that gave the Church the spiritual force to perform her mission. The days when the disciples could be terrorized, as they were after the Master's death, were over; from now on they would serve Christ with a courage that nothing could shake. Neither blows nor tortures nor death itself— nothing would keep them from proclaiming their faith in Jesus the Messias.

The story of their apostolate begins at this very moment. Word of the happening in the Cenacle had gone around and a large crowd had gathered about the house. Someone whispered, "What has happened? Have these men gone mad? What is it that makes them reel as though they have drunk too much wine? And why do they talk in all sorts of strange languages?" Then Peter appeared and made a gesture to silence the crowd. He was no longer the poor man we saw denying his Master for fear of blows and torture. Peter knew no more fear, and now he began to speak:

"Men of Israel, hear these words! Jesus of Nazareth, He who

[1] *The Book of Books,* see chapter VIII.

preached and worked miracles among you, whom wicked men have crucified and slain—this Man, we now tell you, was the Messias, the Son of God made Man, the envoy sent by God to earth to bring salvation to the world. You thought you saw Him die, but He rose from the dead and now reigns in heaven at the right hand of the Father. Let all the people of Israel know that God has made both Lord and Messias this same Jesus, Jesus the Crucified."

It is almost two thousand years, my dear young friends, since these words were spoken, and in the last nineteen centuries the Church has never ceased to repeat them to the world. In obedience to her Master's command, she has ceaselessly preached to mankind the Good News, the Gospel of love and peace. No power has ever been able to silence her, and none ever will. Think back to the first chapter of this book. There we told you of the first centuries of our era, when the Roman emperors tried in every way possible to prevent the spread of Christianity. But nothing could keep the Divine Word from spreading through the world. Hidden in the Catacombs, the early Christians continued to meet and to preach the Gospel. When the pagan executioners tortured them or burned them alive, or threw them to wild beasts in the amphitheaters and circuses of Imperial Rome, they continued to repeat what Peter had declared on the feast of Pentecost: "We believe that Jesus is the Messias, that He came to earth, died and then rose from the dead."

It is a long, long time since these things happened, but the Church of Christ remains. In nineteen centuries she has never failed or ceased to pass on to men, generation by generation, the teachings she received from her Master. She has enabled men to partake of the same Sacraments, of the same "Bread of Life" as were given to her by Jesus. By celebrating the Mass, she enables her children to assist at the very sacrifice that was made on Calvary for the salvation of each and every one of us.

Just think of the courage and heroism that were needed all down the long centuries for the good seed scattered by Jesus to fall on fruitful soil and to produce an abundant harvest. Today there are some seven hundred and eighty-three million Christians in the world, of all races, of all countries, of all tongues. There are even bishops of the black and yellow races; and the name of Jesus is spoken and His Gospel is preached in the heart of the forests of Central Africa as it is amid the Alaskan snows or the islands of Japan. Truly, the Church has fulfilled the mission given to her by her Master, "Teach ye all nations."

Of course, the task is not finished. There are still vast numbers of people on earth who have never heard the name of Jesus Christ. There are also, which is much worse, people among us here in our own country who no longer wish to listen to Jesus' message, who consider His great precept of love as outworn and useless. To all these, including the most ignorant and the most hostile, the Church appeals unceasingly. As her Master taught her in the parable of the Prodigal Son, her arms are opened wide to welcome her ungrateful children in a gesture of love and forgiveness.

There is not one among us who has not known the tenderness of this gesture by which Jesus and His Church have for all these centuries welcomed sinners back into the fold. You already know from your own experience, and you will continue to learn as you grow older, that there are moments in life when we are overcome by grief and sadness and feel that there is no courage or strength left in us. We are crushed under the weight of our sins and ask ourselves how we can regain our happiness. It is in moments such as this, when we kneel and pray in the shadowy interior of some church, that we feel an invisible but infinitely consoling Presence. In the silence there is a Voice which answers our questions, and a gentle hand seems to be laid on our forehead.

We know whose presence this is: it is Jesus who is alway there, always ready to forgive the sins of men. Just as in the days when He cured the blind and the crippled, He asks only one thing of us in order to give us peace again. It is the cry to which He has never turned a deaf ear: "Lord, I believe! Have pity on me!"

Table of Dates

A. D. 27

December   John the Baptist begins his mission.

A. D. 28

January   Jesus is baptized.
February   Jesus' fast in the desert.
March   Miracle of the marriage feast at Cana.
May   John the Baptist is cast into prison.
    Jesus speaks to the Samaritan woman.
    The miraculous draught of fishes.
June   The Sermon on the Mount.
July   Jesus cures the centurion's servant.
December   Jesus calms the tempest.

A. D. 29

March   Death of John the Baptist.
April   The miracle of the loaves and fishes.
July   "Thou art Peter."
August   The Transfiguration.
September   Jesus in Judea.
October   Jesus teaches the "Our Father."

A. D. 30

February   "Suffer the little children to come unto Me."
March   The raising of Lazarus.

HOLY WEEK

Sunday, April 2	Palm Sunday: The entry into Jerusalem.
Tuesday, April 4	Jesus foretells the destruction of Jerusalem.
Wednesday, April 5	Jesus is betrayed by Judas.
Thursday, April 6	The Last Supper: "This is My Body, this is My Blood."
Friday, April 7	The trial, Passion and death of Jesus.
Sunday, April 9	The Resurrection.

LATER DATES

A. D. 50– 55	St. Matthew wrote the first Gospel.
55– 62	St. Mark wrote the second Gospel.
63	St. Luke wrote the third Gospel.
96–104	St. John wrote the fourth Gospel.

An
ARKIVE
EDITION

FROM SOPHIA INSTITUTE PRESS

ARKive Editions are exact photographic reproductions of books published in previous decades or centuries. In them, you find undiluted by modern notions or passing fads the words and ideas of good and thoughtful souls who preceded us in this life.

In this, there is great value: it helps free us from the myopia that afflicts souls drowning in the words and images flooding forth from our modern media, with its attention focused so intently on that which is new and popular today.

Our age is less than perfect and ARKive Editions help us see that, enabling us to measure our own day by the often better standards of other times and places.

At the same time, previous ages and other cultures had their faults: and even in good books from earlier times we often find language, ideas, or values that were once deemed acceptable even by honorable souls, but are now seen clearly to be wrong.

We exclude from ARKive Editions books that have in them as significant themes ideas that are wrong. When, however, books that are overwhelmingly good are tainted by unfortunate peripheral remarks or occasional wrongheaded judgments, we have chosen to publish them intact. For we judge that the good to be done by such books far outweighs the harm done by occasional remarks which good men and women these days can (and should) dismiss as the unfortunate products of an age as flawed as our own, albeit in different ways.

If you disagree with our judgment, please understand, nonetheless, that we have sought to act in goodwill. Let your disagreement be an occasion for you to pray that our generation will soon come to see our own errors as clearly as we see the errors of earlier times; and then turn your attention back to the true riches that are to be found in each of our ARKive Editions, presented here exactly as, they appeared to readers in earlier times.

For your free catalog, contact us at:

Sophia Institute Press®
Box 5284, Manchester, NH 03108
1-800-888-9344

www.SophiaInstitute.com

Sophia Institute® is a tax-exempt institution as defined by the
Internal Revenue Code, Section 501(c)(3). Tax I.D. 22-2548708.

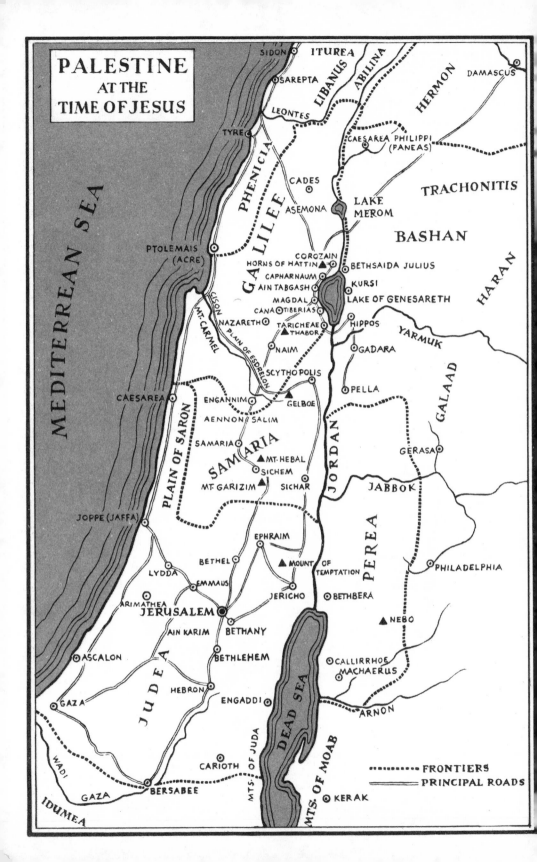

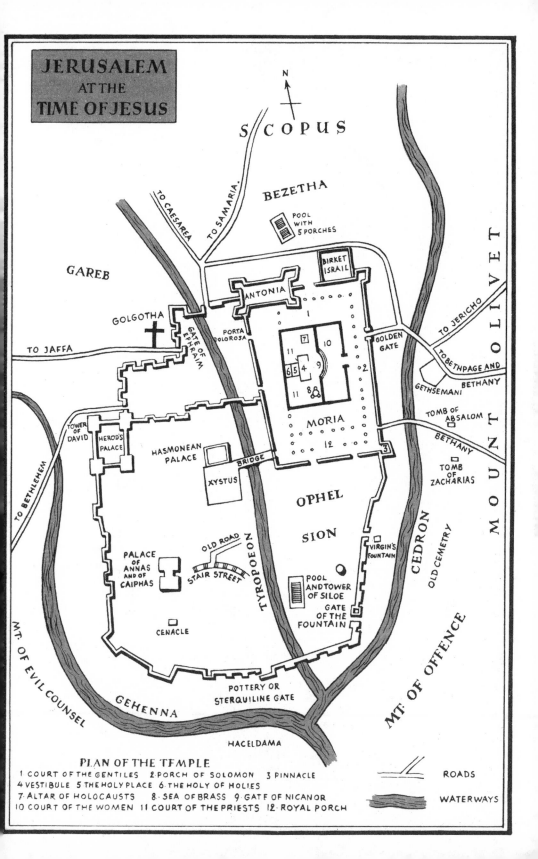

JERUSALEM AT THE TIME OF JESUS

N

S·COPUS

BEZETHA

POOL WITH 5 PORCHES

TO CAESAREA

TO SAMARIA.

GAREB

BIRKET ISRAIL

ANTONIA

GOLGOTHA

GATE OF EPHRAIM

PORTA DOLOROSA

1

7 10

11 6 5 4 9

11 8 8

GOLDEN GATE

TO JAFFA

TO JERICHO

TO BETHPAGE AND BETHANY

GETHSEMANI

MORIA

12

TOMB OF ABSALOM

TOWER OF DAVID

HEROD'S PALACE

HASMONEAN PALACE

XYSTUS

BRIDGE

BETHANY

TOMB OF ZACHARIAS

OPHEL

SION

TO BETHLEHEM

VIRGIN'S FOUNTAIN

OLD CEMETERY

MOUNT OLIVET

CEDRON

PALACE OF ANNAS AND OF CAIPHAS

OLD ROAD

STAIR STREET

TYROPOEON

POOL AND TOWER OF SILOE

CENACLE

GATE OF THE FOUNTAIN

MT. OF OFFENCE

MT. OF EVIL COUNSEL

GEHENNA

POTTERY OR STERQUILINE GATE

HACELDAMA

PLAN OF THE TEMPLE

1 COURT OF THE GENTILES 2·PORCH OF SOLOMON 3 PINNACLE
4 VESTIBULE 5 THE HOLY PLACE 6·THE HOLY OF HOLIES
7· ALTAR OF HOLOCAUSTS 8· SEA OF BRASS 9· GATE OF NICANOR
10 COURT OF THE WOMEN 11 COURT OF THE PRIESTS 12· ROYAL PORCH

ROADS

WATERWAYS